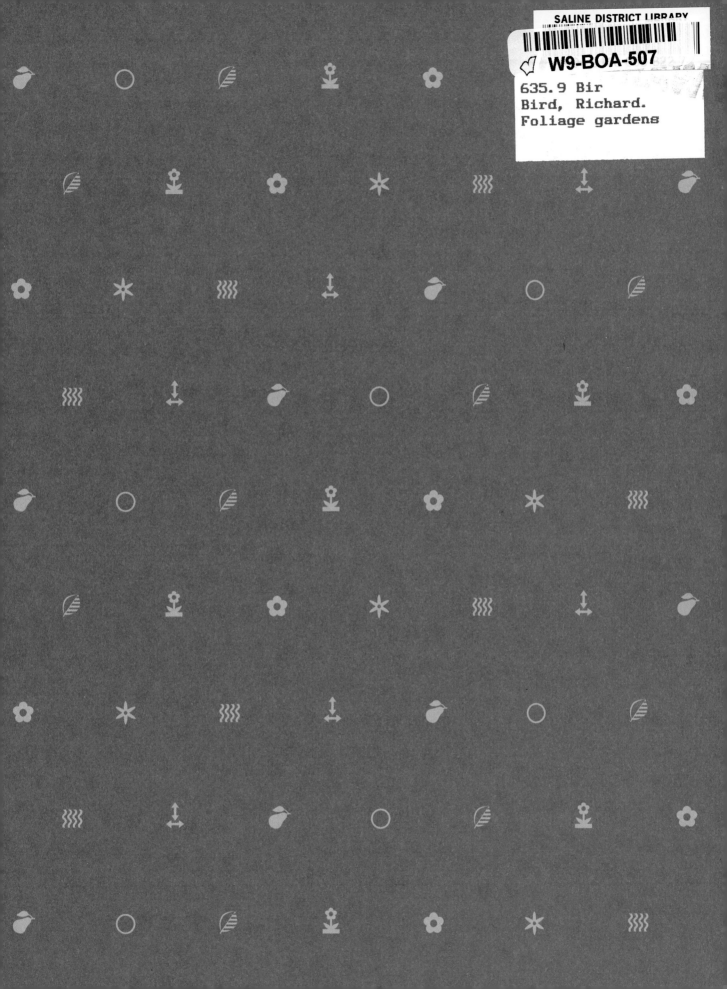

Foliage Gardens

CASSELL'S GARDEN DIRECTORIES

Foliage Gardens

EVERYTHING YOU NEED TO CREATE A GARDEN

RICHARD BIRD

Consultant Editor
LUCY HUNTINGTON

CASSELL&CO

Distributed in the United States of America
by Sterling Publishing Co., Inc.
387 Park Avenue South, New York NY 10016-8810

A CIP Catalogue record for this book is available
from the British Library

ISBN 0 30435807 X

This book was conceived, designed, and produced by

THE IVY PRESS LIMITED
The Old Candlemakers, West Street, Lewes,
East Sussex BN7 2NZ

Creative Director: PETER BRIDGEWATER
Designers: AXIS DESIGN
Editorial Director: SOPHIE COLLINS
Project Editor: ANDREW KIRK
Illustrations: VANESSA LUFF & PETER BULL
Picture Researcher: LIZ EDDISON

Originated and printed in China by Hong Kong Graphic,
Hong Kong

This book is typeset in 10.5/13 Linotype Perpetua and Univers

CASSELL & CO
Wellington House, 125 Strand, London WC2R 0BB

ACKNOWLEDGMENTS

t *top* **b** *below* **l** *left* **r** *right* ***Directory a—f**, starting from top*

A-Z Botanical Collection 88a / Ron Bonser 95a / Bob Gibbons 74c
/ Julia Hancock 91c / David Hughes 84f / K. Jayaram 62b / Dan Sams
100b / Anthony Seinet 104f /
Steven Taylor 106e / Adrian Thomas 66c, 74b,e, 79b / Yves Tzaud 80c /
Chris Wheeler 80f /
A Young 74a;

Liz Eddison 1 & 14b, 6 & 112, 10–11, 12t, 14t, 26–27, 28l,r, 29l,r,
33r, 39, 53, 56, 58–59 / Julian Dowle 17 / Alan Sargent, Chelsea '99
32r / Whichford Pottery 36;

The Garden Picture Library / Philippe Bonduel 94e / Brian Carter
72a / Ron Evans 63b /
John Glover 75a, 96f , 102c/ Neil Holmes 88e / Jacqui Hurst 88d /
Jerry Pavia 81a, 88c, 89d / Howard Rice 62f, 85c, 92d / JS Sira 64b, 65f
/ Didier Willery 68e;

John Glover 2 & 34, 3 & 30l, 7, 12b, 13, 15, 16t, 22, 30r, 31l,r, 32l, 33l,
45, 46, 49, 51, 55, 77f / Bunny Guinness, Chelsea '95 43 / Chris
Jacobsen 16b, 19 / Fiona Lawrenson 4 & 18t /
Karen Maskell, Hampton Court '99 24 / Roger Platts, Chelsea '96 20 /
Tim Stuart-Smith, Chelsea '98 18b / Geoffrey Whiten, Hampton Court
95 41;

Andrew Lawson 70c & 87c;

Peter McHoy 62c, 63a, 64e, 65a,b, 66d,e,f, 68b,c. 70a,f, 71d,f, 72f,
73b,c,d, 74f, 75d,f, 77a,c, 78a,c, 80a,b,e, 81e, 82b,e,f, 84a,b,e, 85a,b,
86c,e, 87a,f, 88b,f, 93c, 94d, 95b,c,e,f, 96a,b,d, 98a, 99b,c,e,f, 100d,
101b, 103f, 105c,d, 107e;

The Harry Smith Collection 62a,d,e, 63c,d,e,f, 64a,c,d,e, 65c,d,e,
66a,b, 67a,b,c,d,e,f, 68a,d,f, 69a,b,d,e,f, 70b,d,e, 71a,b,e, 72b,c,d,e,
73a,f, 74d, 75b,c, 76a,c,d,e,f, 77b,d,e, 78b,d,e, 79a,c,d,e, 80d,
81b,c,d,f, 82a,c,d, 83a,b,c,d,e,f, 84c,d, 85d,e,f, 86a,b,d,f, 87b,d,e,
89a,b,c,f, 90a,b,c,d,e,f, 91a,b,d,e,f, 92a,b,c,e, 93a,b,d,e,f, 94a,b,f, 95d,
96e, 97a,c,d,e,f, 98b,c,d, 99a,d, 100a,f, 101a,c,d,e,f, 102a,b,d,e,f,
103a,b,c,e, 104a,b,c,d,e, 105a,b,e,f, 106a,b,f, 107a,b,c,d,f;

David Squire 69c, 71c, 73e, 75e, 78f, 79f, 94c, 96c, 97b, 98e,f,
100c,e, 103d, 105c,d;

Garden and Wildlife Matters 76b, 92f.

CONTENTS

INTRODUCTION

Foliage is just as important as flowers are in a garden. It forms the backbone and structure around which everything else revolves. Most gardens are planned around flower color alone, with little thought given to leaves and the contribution they make. Yet, once the diversity and excitement of the many leaf shapes, sizes, textures, and colors are appreciated, it soon becomes apparent that there are wonderful combinations and plant associations to be explored. Foliage provides interest in its own right, as well as offering a foil or background against which flowers and other features can be displayed to advantage.

Planning a garden around plants selected for their leaves can be extremely rewarding and does not prevent you including flowers as a seasonal bonus. In fact, there is no real war between foliage and flowers; they both make a great contribution to our gardens and both are indispensable. Foliage can stand on its own but it also works beautifully in combination with flowers.

Foliage has everything to offer. It has shape, texture, and color. Although there is not a huge range of color, foliage color tends to form broad sweeps rather than the individual brush-strokes that flowers offer, presenting a more subtle approach to color. There is such variety that most designs can be accomplished with few problems, and foliage is much simpler to combine than flowers.

THEN AND NOW

❧ While many flowering plants have altered beyond recognition over the centuries, many foliage plants would still be easily recognizable by our gardening ancestors.
❧ In some cases it is the individual plants that have remained unchanged. Some yews (*Taxus baccata*), for example, have graced the same gardens for literally hundreds of years.

APPEALING TO THE SENSES

Leaves have a greater appeal to our senses than flowers. You can look at flowers, you can smell them, and you can taste some of them by eating them. All three of these senses can also be applied to foliage, but so can two others. Foliage can create a restful sound in a garden. Tall grasses hissing together, the trembling leaves of the aspen, and the rustling of dry beech leaves in winter all create a pleasant background. Leaves are also very tactile. Few people walk past a rosemary bush or a soft yew hedge, for example, without running their fingers through them. Soft grasses and felted leaves are also extremely inviting to the touch.

A GREEN OASIS

In the countryside there is likely to be a great deal of natural foliage effects from surrounding trees, hedges, and fields. In the town, on the other hand, buildings and traffic are likely to predominate. You can escape to a local park, but

LEFT *Different shades of green foliage can be used to superb effect to create a backdrop against which to show off the bright, exhilarating colors of spring and summer flowers.*

to have your own private oasis of greenery is a luxury that is relatively simple to achieve. A lot of foliage in a garden not only provides a refuge for busy people, it also acts as a life-saver for many birds and insects, providing shelter and nesting sites, as well as food. Even rural villages are becoming more built up, and their centers are often as congested as any town. The need for pockets of greenery where people can breathe has never been greater.

EVERGREEN FOLIAGE

The leaves on most plants far outlive the flowers. However, the doyen of longevity must be the evergreens on which leaves seem to remain forever. In fact they are regularly replaced, but their individual demise is not often noticed. The advantage of evergreen plants is that they give permanent structure to a garden. They also need very little attention, particularly as (unless they are in the form of a hedge or topiary) they need very little pruning. Care must

ABOVE *Use a mixture of foliage types in a border to give variety in shape and texture. A bonus with some good foliage plants is that they also produce dramatic displays of blooms.*

be taken, however, to prevent evergreens dominating the deciduous foliage in a garden as they can create a cold, slightly empty feeling. They can also lead to boredom if the scene never changes, but when they are mixed with deciduous plants much more liveliness and variation can be introduced and they play an important role.

USING FOLIAGE

This book examines all the different types of foliage and how they react to each other and to flowers. It looks at how to plan a garden and achieve a range of attractive garden features using foliage. Most importantly, it includes a large directory of handsome foliage plants, with detailed descriptions and suggested uses.

HOW TO USE THIS BOOK

*C*assell's Garden Directories have been conceived and written to appeal both to gardening beginners and to confident gardeners who need advice for a specific project. Each book focuses on a particular type of garden, drawing on the experience of an established expert. The emphasis is on a practical and down-to-earth approach that takes account of the space, time, and money that you have available. The ideas and techniques in these books will help you to produce an attractive and manageable garden that you will enjoy for years to come.

Foliage Gardens introduces the huge and varied array of foliage types available to gardeners and suggests creative ways to use this often undervalued resource. The book is divided into three sections. The opening section, Planning your Garden, introduces the subject of foliage, looking at the subtle and stunning effects that can be achieved and the range of foliage plants that is available. There is a section covering planning a complete foliage garden, as well as three specific inspirational garden plans for using foliage in different ways.

Part Two of the book, entitled Creating your Garden, moves on to the nitty-gritty of selecting, buying, and planting foliage plants. This section opens with a description of some of the different leaf shapes, leaf sizes, and leaf textures that can be used to great effect in the garden, with a list of suggested plants that you can choose from.

The remainder of Part Two is packed with practical information on acquiring the plants, as well as basic techniques for sowing seeds, dividing plants, and taking cuttings, and how to prepare the soil and care for your foliage plants after planting. Moving on from this basic grounding, this section then encourages you to put your skills to work with a series of specific projects, such as making a lavender path, planting a barrel pond, creating a mop-headed bay tree, and planting a thick foliage hedge to screen the garden from unwanted noise. There are step-by-step illustrations throughout this section that show clearly and simply what you need to do to achieve the best results. Also included are handy hints and tips, points to watch out for, and star plants that are particularly suitable for the projects that are described.

The final part of the book, The Plant Directory, comprises a comprehensive listing of all the plants that have been mentioned and recommended in the earlier sections, together with other eye-catching foliage plants. Each plant is illustrated in color, and comprehensive information on appropriate growing conditions, speed of growth, and ease of maintenance has been supplied throughout.

GARDEN SCHEMES *are included to inspire you to great things in your own garden.*

COLOR PHOTOGRAPHS *show what can be achieved with a little effort and imagination.*

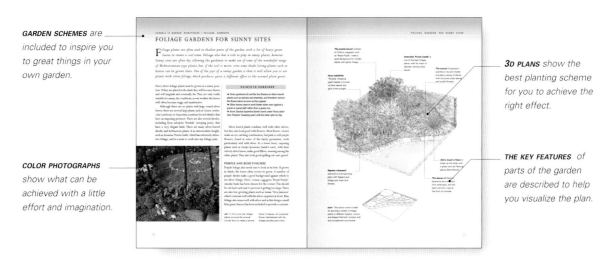

3D PLANS *show the best planting scheme for you to achieve the right effect.*

THE KEY FEATURES *of parts of the garden are described to help you visualize the plan.*

CHOICES SPREADS show a selection of very different plants with interesting foliage that might be appropriate in your garden.

COLOR PHOTOGRAPHS help you to decide on the appropriate feature for your garden.

EXPLANATORY TEXT describes the various possibilities available in each category.

THE CHECKLIST details important things to look out for in choosing garden features.

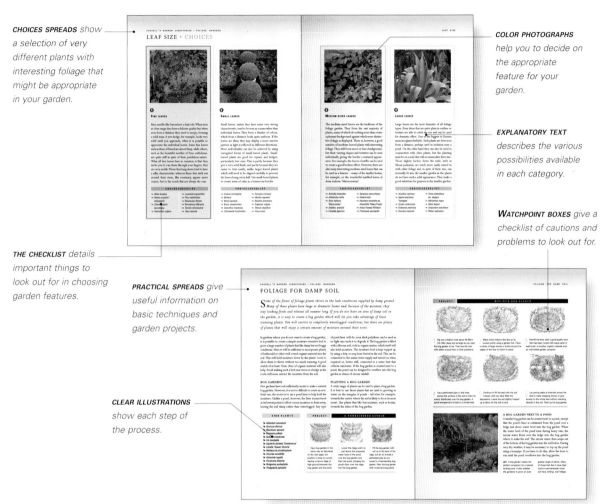

WATCHPOINT BOXES give a checklist of cautions and problems to look out for.

PRACTICAL SPREADS give useful information on basic techniques and garden projects.

CLEAR ILLUSTRATIONS show each step of the process.

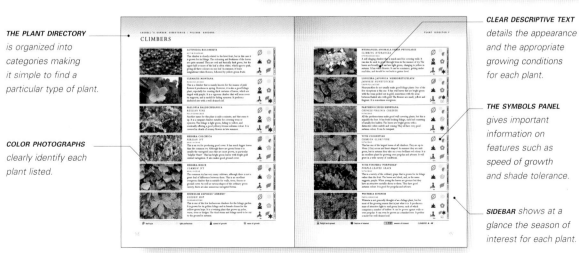

THE PLANT DIRECTORY is organized into categories making it simple to find a particular type of plant.

CLEAR DESCRIPTIVE TEXT details the appearance and the appropriate growing conditions for each plant.

COLOR PHOTOGRAPHS clearly identify each plant listed.

THE SYMBOLS PANEL gives important information on features such as speed of growth and shade tolerance.

SIDEBAR shows at a glance the season of interest for each plant.

1

PLANNING YOUR GARDEN

While it can be fun just to pop plants into gaps without giving any thought to the overall design of the garden, a much more satisfactory result will be accomplished through careful planning. First think about what you want to achieve in terms of general features and style, and then consider how to go about it. You do not have to be an artist or master draftsman to plan a garden. Clear thinking, lists, and rough sketches are all that most gardeners use.

LEFT *At the planning stage, think about which foliage plants will complement each other—here euphorbias and hardy geraniums make perfect partners.*

LEAF VARIETIES

*O*ne of the main attractions of foliage is its sheer diversity. There is an extensive range of different leaf shapes, colors, and textures. The ultimate shape of the plant also has a distinctive effect, whether it is an upright fountain, a rounded hummock, or a ground-hugging carpet. All these factors combine to produce a stunning array of highly individual plant forms, offering scope for exciting and unusual plant combinations.

The impact of foliage is threefold. First, there is the intrinsic nature of the individual leaf. A particular leaf may create an interesting image, such as the filigree effect of a fern leaf. Secondly, there is the total effect of all the leaves on one plant. For example, fern leaves all emerge from a central point to form a neat fountain of foliage. Finally, there is the interplay of one set of leaves with another, demonstrated by the way an upright filigree fern contrasts with the solid mass of a mound of rounded hosta leaves.

LEAF SHAPE AND SIZE

There is tremendous diversity in leaf shape and size, from the long, strap-like leaves of *Phormium tenax* (New Zealand flax) to the softly divided leaves of astilbes, and from the huge jagged leaves of *Rheum palmatum* (ornamental rhubarb) to the tiny leaves of *Buxus sempervirens* (box) which is so perfect for topiary. Each type of foliage is suitable for a different role in a garden, whether it is to create a bold focal point, form a living barrier, or provide a lush background to set off other plants.

The shapes of leaves are most noticeable when they are outlined against the sky. Maple leaves, for example, look particularly stunning in silhouette, and it is important that you should be able to walk under such a tree. On the other hand, it is the sheer size of *Gunnera manicata* (giant rhubarb) leaves that is most interesting, and these are best appreciated when you stand under them. So it is always essential to locate plants with interesting foliage where it can be seen to best advantage, otherwise a crucial element in their attraction is lost.

EFFECTS OF TEXTURE

Texture is often the least recognized attribute of foliage plants, yet it has a huge effect on the look of the plant. Texture has two aspects. The first is the texture of the leaf. Some leaves are glossy and shiny (*Camellia japonica*, for example), others matte (*Geranium macrorrhizum*), and yet others felted, such as the furry leaves of *Stachys byzantina* (lamb's ears). In some cases, it is not so much the texture of the leaf as its appearance. For example, many hosta leaves have a pleated or puckered effect which influences their look. The second aspect of texture is the effect the leaves give to the overall plant. Some shrubs, such as rosemary, look soft and luxurious despite having quite stiff leaves, while others have a harder, more formal appearance.

LEFT *Leaves are not just plain green and medium in size. Some are small and purplish,* *creating a dark background; others are large, striped, and bold, standing out in style.*

Texture also plays an important part in plant association. A mixture of textures within a border creates a stimulating scene and adds another dimension to that of color or shape alone. Leaves are often matte or glossy on top and hairy or furry underneath, and when these twist in the wind they cause a vibrant effect. Shiny or glossy foliage is important in a mixed scheme as it will glisten and reflect light, which is especially valuable in dark areas.

OVERALL HABIT

The overall shape of a plant is a crucial factor in its appearance and the way it is used within a planting scheme, and it is usually the foliage that dictates this. The fountain effect of the sword- and strap-like foliage of such plants as *Cordyline*, *Hemerocallis*, *Iris*, *Phormium*, and *Yucca* is produced by the leaves. Other plants have a horizontal arrangement of foliage, including many conifers such as *Juniperus horizontalis*. This creates a blanketing effect, useful for providing

POINTS TO CONSIDER

❧ Not all leaves are interesting. Some are quite ordinary to look at, but they can still act as useful fillers.

❧ You should use plants with bold foliage sparingly to create dramatic effects.

❧ Do not forget how important silhouettes can be and, if possible, aim to display some foliage against the sky or other light background such as a white-painted wall.

a horizontal accent and creating a strong contrast with upright plants. Another such plant is *Cornus controversa* 'Variegata' (wedding cake tree) whose branches are arranged in distinctive tiers. In contrast, many herbaceous plants, such as hostas and geraniums, create rounded mounds of foliage which usually provide the main bulk of a border and set off the upright plants; and others form a flat carpet, including *Lysimachia nummularia* and the ajugas.

All these habits interplay with one another to create a complete picture. A sea of rounded hostas is boring, but when broken up with a few clumps of upright irises or carpeting ajugas it becomes much more interesting.

COLORED FOLIAGE

There is a tendency to think of leaves as simply being green, but if you look carefully you will realize just what a vast spectrum of greens exists. There are also several other colors found in foliage, from variegated plants with reds, yellows, golds, whites, and silvers in stripes or blotches on the green background to self-colored leaves in rich purples, cool blues, dazzling golds, soft misty grays, and startling silvers.

Whatever foliage you use in the garden, green will always be the basic color, the one used to unify and set off all the others. Yet the variation in greens is enormous and the different shades will create different feelings. Lime-green, for example, is dazzling and brings a modern feel. A few *Tanacetum parthenium* 'Aureum' (golden feverfew) plants dotted around in a foliage border will add a spring-like quality all summer. Somber dark greens, on the other hand, lend an old-fashioned or formal feel. Spring is the best time to appreciate green leaves, as they are soft and fresh when they emerge. As summer progresses, they become "tired" and tend to merge into a more uniform green, but even then there are many variations with which to experiment.

WHITE AND GREEN VARIEGATED LEAVES
The green parts of a plant contain chlorophyll, which transforms the sun's energy into simple sugars for growth. There are no pure white leaves, as a plant cannot survive without

chlorophyll, but there are plants with partially white leaves, and these have great impact. They may be striped, like *Phalaris arundinacea* var. *picta* (gardener's garters), or have white blotches or patches, seen in many hostas and *Phlox paniculata* 'Norah Leigh', for example. These plants are good for lighting up a dull corner, as they shine out.

YELLOW LEAVES AND VARIEGATIONS
Although pure white cannot exist on its own as a foliage color, yellow can. This is because there is always an underlying hint of green in yellow leaves. Frequently, many yellow-leaved plants (hostas are a typical example) turn greener as the season progresses. On the other hand, the many yellow-variegated plants hold their color until they drop. Again the variegations can be in the form of stripes, blotches, or patches. Like the white and green variegated plants, yellow-leaved plants and variegations are good for illuminating shade. Examples include *Acer shirasawanum*

LEFT Cerinthe major 'Purpurascens' is a hardy annual with steely-blue foliage. It contrasts well with the golden strap-like foliage of the grass Hakonechloa macra 'Alboaurea'.

'Aureum' (golden Japanese maple), *Philadelphus coronarius* 'Aureus' (golden philadelphus), *Milium effusum* 'Aureum' (Bowles' golden grass), and *Aucuba japonica* 'Variegata' (spotted laurel).

PURPLE AND PLUM LEAVES

There is a surprising number of purple-leaved plants, including *Cotinus coggygria* 'Royal Purple' (smoke bush) and *Ajuga reptans* 'Atropurpurea' (bugle). When looked at closely, however, they reveal that green is never far away. Some purple-leaved plants are only suited to sunny sites as the purple may fade and revert to green in a shady position. Purple should be used sparingly; too much in a border or garden has a leaden effect on the planting and becomes heavy and rather dull. A few well-placed purple-leaved plants can have a dramatic effect, though, especially if planted so that the evening light shines through the leaves.

BLUE AND GLAUCOUS LEAVES

There are few really blue leaves, although some plants get very near to it, such as *Acaena* 'Blue Haze', *Festuca glauca* (blue fescue), and *Hosta sieboldiana* var. *elegans*. Like the purples, they can become a little heavy if planted in quantity, so use them to make a statement rather than a general planting. Blue foliage combines particularly well with lime-green for a very contemporary contrast.

SILVER LEAVES

There are two types of silver-leaved plants: those with truly silver leaves (such as cyclamens, *Lamium galeobdolon,* and *Pulmonaria saccharata*) and those whose leaves are covered with fine white hairs, giving an overall silver appearance. Examples of the latter include *Stachys byzantina* (lamb's ears). The fine hairs on these plants are designed to protect against moisture loss, indicating that these plants have evolved to cope with hot, dry conditions and will not do well in shade. Silver foliage is dramatic and, although these plants make a fine addition to a foliage border, they also mix extremely well with a wide range of flower colors, especially pastel shades of pink, blue, and yellow.

BELOW *Conifers and heathers grown together can produce pleasing combinations of form and color. Some conifers have bluish or glaucous foliage that . offsets brighter greens nicely.*

EFFECTIVE USE OF FOLIAGE

Foliage can be used to create a number of different impressions within a garden setting. Lush, large-leaved plants create a tranquil, leafy oasis, while clipped small-leaved shrubs can bring a formal note in the form of smart hedges and even topiary. A tapestry of rich greens and blues in a shady spot will create quite a cool feel, while a mixture of silver- and colored-leaved shrubs will add extra warmth to a sunny corner.

Green is a very peaceful color. It is all-pervasive, lush, and calming. When you are feeling stressed, try walking through a wood and notice how this relieves tension and lifts the spirits. Transfer that wood to your garden in the form of foliage plants, even if it is only a bower of green leaves in a small back yard, and you will get some of the same stress-relieving effects. The subtle variations in foliage plants, especially when used in shade, are generally much more restful to the eye than any flower combination and this alone makes for a tranquil scene. Perhaps some of the excitement is missing, but that can be introduced in the

form of texture, leaf color and autumn tints, and of course by the careful use of flowering plants among the foliage. A foliage garden does not have to exclude flowers.

You can create tranquillity by using density of leaves to absorb the noise of traffic and neighbors. Foliage can create a hideaway where it is possible to find solitude.

CREATING COOLNESS

Green is not only a tranquil color but also a cool one. This is partly a property of the color itself, but also has much to do with the fact that a canopy of green foliage creates a shadow. The shade created by many foliage plants, especially trees and large shrubs, means that the soil beneath them is permanently moist, and this in turn creates a damp, cool atmosphere. This makes foliage gardens cool, comfortable places to be in warm weather, which you will know if you have ever eaten lunch under a vine-covered pergola in midsummer.

LEFT Foliage can be useful as well as decorative. Here herbs and a variety of other plants used in aromatherapy create a delightful visual and fragrant display while they are growing.

CREATING WARMTH

Not all foliage plants are cool, however. Some, particularly those with golden leaves or variegation, are much warmer and introduce an element of brightness. These can be used in sun or shade to the same effect, but they will obviously shine out in a dark corner. Much can be done to set the mood of the garden by careful choice of plants. Silver-leaved plants and those with leathery foliage can give a Mediterranean feel to a sunny patch, especially when planted in a gravel garden. These include *Artemisia ludoviciana*, *Convolvulus cneorum*, lavender, rosemary, *Salvia argentea* (silver salvia), and *Sedum spectabile* (ice plant).

LOW MAINTENANCE

Most foliage plants need far less attention than those grown specifically for their flowers. The most maintenance-free are the evergreen trees and shrubs which need little, if any, pruning. As a bonus, the mere fact that plants are grown for their foliage often means that the leaf cover is quite dense, thus making it difficult for weeds to become established underneath them. Foliage plants also make ideal ground cover, filling an area of soil with handsome foliage and suppressing the growth of weeds. There is no such thing as a totally maintenance-free garden, but one of the closest must be a complete covering of *Hedera helix* (ivy) which romps over logs, hillocks, and other objects to create interesting undulations and patterns. It only needs clipping over once a year in spring, and will grow in dry shade, a problem place for most plants. There are other plants, however, that perhaps make more interesting ground cover. These include *Aguja reptans* (bugle), which comes in many leaf colors including a deep purple and a highly variegated form with pink and white patches, and *Lamium maculatum* (deadnettle) which also comes in a variety of leaf colors, many with silver markings. Both produce handsome flowers throughout the summer months.

ENHANCING GARDEN FEATURES

While foliage can be clipped into regular shapes, it can also be left to grow in an unrestrained manner. This can be useful when creating a wild garden, but it can also be used in a more formal way to enhance other features in the garden. Many garden structures, such as sheds, summer-

ABOVE *Garden ornaments need not stand alone. They can be clothed with plants that have interesting foliage or flowers, or both. Use some evergreens to maintain interest during winter.*

houses, arbors and so on are very angular in their design and construction. Unless in a stark, modern setting, this contrasts unfavorably with the softer lines of a garden. Foliage plants can be used to enhance these structures, softening their hard lines and covering any plain areas. Climbing plants, in particular, are useful for this purpose, but shrubs can also be used to grow up against a shed or fence. Other types of garden feature, such as garden ornaments, will often benefit from a careful use of foliage. Statues, for example, look good when set against a dark, formal hedge, or can be enhanced with a few well-placed trails of a climber such as *Hedera helix* (ivy).

There are times when certain features, such as an ugly garage or row of dustbins, need to be hidden completely. Again foliage plants, especially evergreen varieties, can be used to great effect. Shrubs can be used to screen such features, and climbing plants such as clematis can be trained over or in front of them to distract the eye.

PLANNING WITH FOLIAGE PLANTS

Foliage plants can be difficult to place, because their subtle effects are harder to visualize than the mixing of flower colors. To get the best results, it is important to think about what you are trying to achieve. The best preparation is to look at as many gardens as you can in order to see how foliage works in different situations. Once you are hooked on foliage and appreciate its many qualities, the rewards will be great.

When combining foliage plants in a garden, the most important aspects to consider are the overall shapes and habits of the plants and the way they relate to each other. For this reason, it is vital to think of the space in three dimensions, rather than making a plan on a sheet of paper that views the garden from above. If you simply look down on the plot, all you see are the basic plant outlines with no concept of how they will really react to one another.

The first approach is to make an overall plan of the area, whether it is a single border or the whole garden. Draw the parameters on a piece of paper, including the hedges, fences, buildings, and any existing trees. Using this as a framework, sketch in where the main groupings of plants will be. Next add seating or activity areas and draw in the lawns and paths. Having got the overall plan it is time to look more closely at the detailed design, moving to ground level to plan it in three dimensions.

OVERALL OUTLINE

Although we move around a garden and see it from all angles, there are generally one or two positions from which the garden is most frequently seen. These may well be from a window or door of the house, or the garden gate. The first sighting is often crucial to the way you see and remember a garden. These are the positions from which to create the general outline. From these points the garden will meander away, with perhaps a progression of taller elements to carry the eye down to the farthest corner. There may be low-growing plants in the foreground and medium-height shrubs to block the view to certain areas to make them more mysterious and create the desire to go and explore.

INDIVIDUAL AREAS

Having worked out the overall shape, it is now time to look at specific areas. Work on one at a time, sketch in any trees and shrubs you want to use and then fill in the gaps. Unless you have specific plants in mind, use stylized outlines to get some idea of how the shapes will work—fuzzy outlines for rounded bushes and arching lines for a fountain-shaped plant, for example. It does not matter if your drawing is neither accurate nor pretty. It is only a guide for yourself and not a work of art to be shown to others.

SELECTING PLANTS

When you have a basic outline of what you are trying to create and have planned the sizes and shapes of plants you need, it is time to select the specific plants. Take into consideration whether the area receives direct sunshine at

LEFT *A complicated formal knot garden like this one will involve a lot of work at the design and planning stages. It will also need a lot of attention in the early stages after planting.*

any time of the day or whether it is constantly shady. If it is shady, you will need to determine the nature of the shade, dappled or deep, and choose the plants accordingly. Also bear in mind the type of soil you have. If it is particularly wet, dry, or chalky, for example, you will need to choose plants that enjoy those conditions.

FINALIZING THE PLAN

Having worked it all out in profile so that you can see the effect you will eventually achieve, and chosen the plants you want to use, it is time to lay it out on a measured drawing to see whether it will all fit. Using squared paper, accurately draw in the outline of the area and fill in the bare bones of the lawns, paths, borders, and other features. Now fill in the plants, placing them in the positions you want them and being as accurate as you can to the eventual size they will make. Obviously with trees that take a hundred years or more to reach their ultimate size it is better to think in terms of twenty years. Some plants will overlap, especially under taller trees. You may have to come to a compromise between the effect you want to create

ABOVE *Informality may look unplanned, but this is often not the case. To achieve an effect like this, you will need to take the plants' height, form, color and texture into consideration.*

and the space you have. In some cases you will have far too many plants; in others the space will look decidedly empty. It may be possible to reduce the number of plants without changing the effect, or increase or decrease the size of the borders to compensate.

POINTS TO CONSIDER

🍃 Try to keep existing trees and shrubs if you can, as they will make the scheme mature more quickly. However, if they are not suitable it is best not to compromise, but to start afresh to create the effect you really want.

🍃 Removal of trees may need planning approval.

🍃 When you get to the planting stage, lay out the plants, still in their pots, and try to imagine the scene when all is fully grown. If necessary, make adjustments to the scheme before planting to avoid having to rectify mistakes later.

THE GREEN OASIS

*O*ne *of the basic functions of a garden, especially in a town setting, is to act as a haven
from the hurry-skurry of everyday life. Foliage plants are ideal for creating such an
oasis, as they instill a feeling of calm and tranquillity. It should be borne in mind that trees
and shrubs do not grow as fast as annuals or herbaceous perennial plants, and the complete
plan may take several years before it eventually comes to fruition. It will be speeded up,
however, if there are existing mature plants that can be incorporated into the plan.*

To achieve a complete oasis away from the world, the
garden must be cut off from external noise and intrusion.
To this end it is important to start off with tall foliage
around the boundaries. In a small garden, this can mean
creating hedges or, as shown here, covering existing fences
with leafy climbers. In a larger garden where a green oasis
is to form just part of the overall area, the glade can be
surrounded by shrubs to make it less formal.

CREATING SHADE
Shade is not essential but it helps to create a cool, relaxing
atmosphere. There will, of course, be shade underneath
the arbor in the plan, but there are also sufficient trees to
create shade within the oasis as a whole. The trees should
not be too dense as dappled shade is preferable to deep.
This is partly because it creates a more pleasant atmosphere and partly because there are not many plants that

will grow in dense shade, whereas dappled shade is more
accommodating. Choose small trees such as *Betula pendula*
(silver birch) or *Pyrus salicifolia* 'Pendula'.

CLOTHING THE ARBOR
The arbor should be covered with climbers, to give it a
gothic and attractive appearance, and to create an enclosed,
leafy bower in which to sit. A "green" room is perfect for
whiling away a summer's day. The area in front of the arbor
could be paved, but gravel or grass would be softer and
more in keeping with the informal aspect of the design.

FILLING IN THE GAPS
The bare bones described above may create an oasis, but
it is the smaller plants that will provide an intimate and
decorative environment. Aim to create a lush tapestry of
foliage, mixing shrubs and perennials with varied shapes,
colors, textures, and forms. Combine ferns with hostas,
rodgersia with acanthus, for a scheme with visual impact.

LEFT *A combination of lush
greens produces a wonderful
feeling of calm. In a small
space, you can use tall plants,
or climbers on fences or poles,
to add height to the planting.*

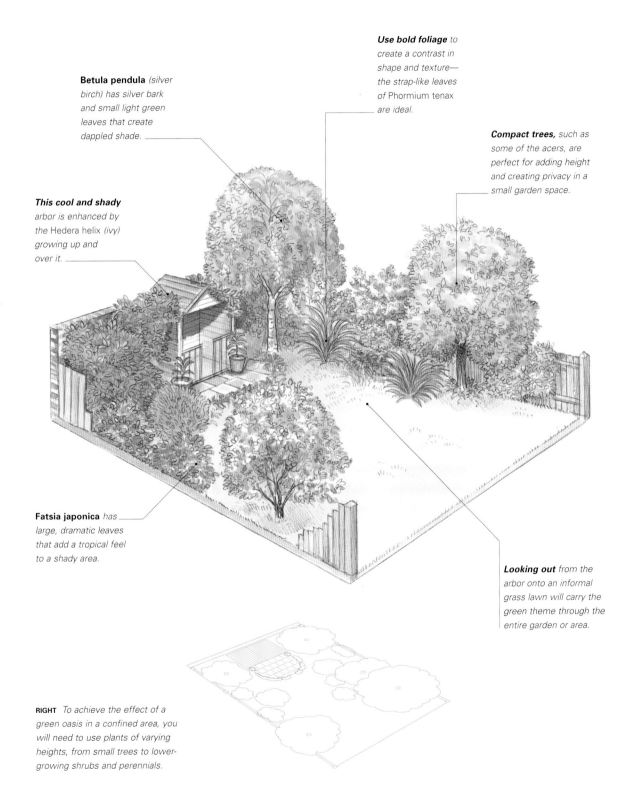

Use bold foliage to create a contrast in shape and texture—the strap-like leaves of Phormium tenax are ideal.

Betula pendula (silver birch) has silver bark and small light green leaves that create dappled shade.

Compact trees, such as some of the acers, are perfect for adding height and creating privacy in a small garden space.

This cool and shady arbor is enhanced by the Hedera helix (ivy) growing up and over it.

Fatsia japonica has large, dramatic leaves that add a tropical feel to a shady area.

Looking out from the arbor onto an informal grass lawn will carry the green theme through the entire garden or area.

RIGHT To achieve the effect of a green oasis in a confined area, you will need to use plants of varying heights, from small trees to lower-growing shrubs and perennials.

A BASEMENT GARDEN

*B*asement gardens can be difficult spaces to cope with as they are often very shady with only brief glimpses of the sun. With ingenuity, however, a garden can be created in such a place, making use of some of the beautiful foliage plants on offer. Any plants you choose must be able to cope with shady conditions, and any hope of a "jungle" effect will be dashed because there would not be sufficient light. A further consideration is that basements are usually paved, with no access to the natural soil, so the plants must be grown in pots.

The first priority when planning a basement garden is to increase the amount of light available. The simplest way of achieving this is to paint all the walls white. This will cause them to reflect light back into the space rather than to absorb it. A pale floor will also help; black asphalt will not. Another way of increasing light levels is to use mirrors. These have two purposes. In the first place, like white paint, they will reflect light back into the space. In the second, the reflection in the mirror will give the impression that the basement is bigger than it actually is. Mirrors are often usefully placed opposite a window, so that when you look out you get the illusion of a bigger view than there is in reality. Preferably it should be positioned at a slight angle so that you do not see the window, and it should be surrounded with soft vegetation to blur its edges.

LEFT *In a shaded area such as a basement garden, a beautiful display can still be achieved by using shade-tolerant foliage plants. If there is not much open soil, grow them in pots.*

POINTS TO CONSIDER

🍂 Climbers should be trained up a wooden trellis which is attached to the wall with hinges at the bottom and catches at the top. The trellis can then be angled away from the wall when you want to paint behind the climbers.

🍂 You can train fine climbing plants across the top of the basement area, but it is generally best to avoid making the space darker by creating a ceiling of foliage.

🍂 Move exotic houseplants, in their pots, outside during the summer months to brighten up the foliage effect.

USING CONTAINERS

If there is no open soil in the basement, choose a selection of interesting pots, boxes, or containers in which to grow the plants. These should reflect the style of the plants and the garden you are aiming to create. Pot-grown plants are easy to maintain, as long as you keep them watered.

ILLUMINATING CORNERS

Any foliage plants are suitable for this, although since there is plenty of wall space there may be a preponderance of climbers. Because of the darkness of many basement areas, it is a good idea to use a few plants with shiny leaves, such as camellias, which will reflect back the light. Similarly, variegated or yellow-leaved plants such as *Humulus lupulus* 'Aureus' (golden hop) will lighten the atmosphere. Do not use too many variegated plants, and if possible site them against plain green plants to show them off to best advantage. Position them out of direct sun to avoid leaf scorch.

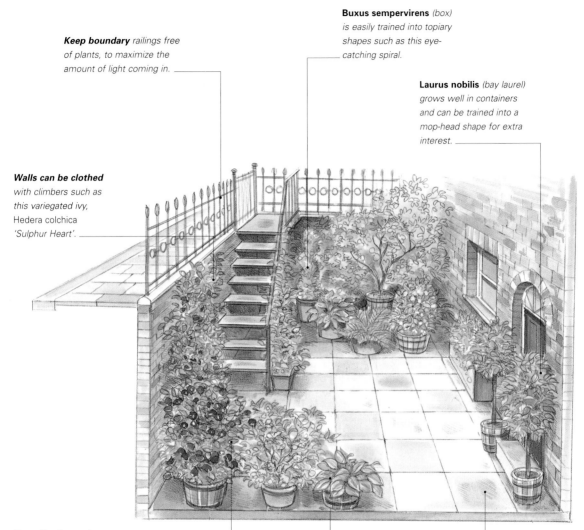

Keep boundary *railings free of plants, to maximize the amount of light coming in.*

Buxus sempervirens *(box) is easily trained into topiary shapes such as this eye-catching spiral.*

Laurus nobilis *(bay laurel) grows well in containers and can be trained into a mop-head shape for extra interest.*

Walls can be clothed *with climbers such as this variegated ivy, Hedera colchica 'Sulphur Heart'.*

Camellias have *glossy dark green leaves all year round and bear attractive flowers in the spring.*

This variegated hosta, *'Frances Williams', is excellent for brightening up a dull corner.*

Paving in a pale color *will help to increase the amount of light in the garden by reflecting rather than absorbing it.*

RIGHT *With a basement garden, it is essential to choose the right plants for the shady conditions. Growing them in containers means they can be moved around to suit.*

23

FOLIAGE GARDENS FOR SUNNY SITES

Foliage plants are often used in shadier parts of the garden, with a lot of heavy green leaves to create a cool scene. Foliage also has a role to play in sunny places, however. Sunny sites are often dry, allowing the gardener to make use of some of the wonderful range of Mediterranean-type plants; but, if the soil is moist, even some shade-loving plants such as hostas can be grown there. One of the joys of a sunny garden is that it will allow you to use plants with silver foliage, which produces quite a different effect to the normal plain green.

Furry silver-foliage plants must be grown in a sunny position. If they are placed in the shade they will become drawn and will languish and eventually die. They are only really suitable for sunny, dry conditions; in wet weather the leaves will often become soggy and unattractive.

Although there are no plants with huge round silver leaves, there are several large plants, such as *Cynara cardunculus* (cardoon) or *Onopordum acanthium* (Scotch thistle) that have an imposing presence. There are also several shrubs, including *Pyrus salicifolia* 'Pendula' (weeping pear), that have a very elegant habit. There are many silver-leaved shrubs and herbaceous plants of an intermediate height, such as *Artemisia* 'Powis Castle' which has extremely attractive foliage, and is a must to work into any foliage plan.

POINTS TO CONSIDER

- Some gardeners do not like the flowers on silver-leaved plants such as stachys and artemisia, and therefore remove the flower stems as soon as they appear.
- Silver leaves seem to work better when seen against a gravel or paved path rather than a grass one.
- Grow *Stachys byzantina* (lamb's ears) under *Pyrus salicifolia* 'Pendula' (weeping pear) until the latter gets too big.

Silver-leaved plants combine well with other silvers, but they also look good with flowers. Most flower colors make an eye-catching combination, but pink or soft purple flowers, found in some of the hardy geraniums, work particularly well with silver. At a lower level, carpeting plants such as *Stachys byzantina* (lamb's ears), with their velvety silver leaves, make good fillers, weaving among the other plants. They also look good spilling out onto gravel.

PURPLE AND BLUE TOUCHES

Purple foliage also needs sun to look at its best. If grown in shade, the leaves often revert to green. A number of purple shrubs make a good background against which to set silver foliage. Here, *Cotinus coggygyria* 'Royal Purple' (smoke bush) has been chosen for the corner. This should be cut back each year to prevent it getting too large. There are also low-growing plants such as *Sedum* 'Vera Jameson' which contrasts well with the silver carpeters in front. Blue foliage also mixes well with silver and in this design a small blue grass (*Festuca*) has been included to provide a contrast.

LEFT *In this sunny site, foliage plants surround the unusual circular lawn to create a "picture frame" of leaves. An occasional flower interspersed with the foliage provides spot color.*

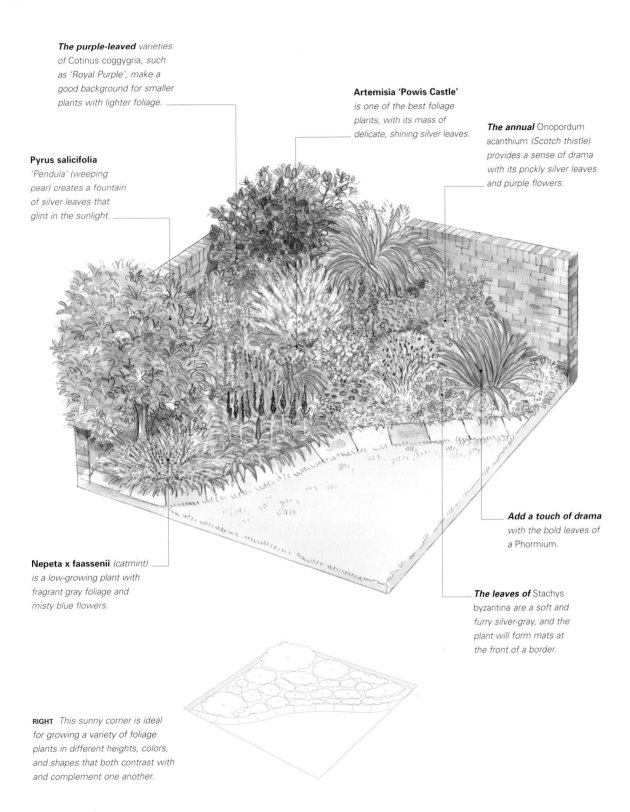

The purple-leaved varieties of Cotinus coggygria, such as 'Royal Purple', make a good background for smaller plants with lighter foliage.

Artemisia 'Powis Castle' is one of the best foliage plants, with its mass of delicate, shining silver leaves.

The annual Onopordum acanthium (Scotch thistle) provides a sense of drama with its prickly silver leaves and purple flowers.

Pyrus salicifolia 'Pendula' (weeping pear) creates a fountain of silver leaves that glint in the sunlight.

Add a touch of drama with the bold leaves of a Phormium.

Nepeta x faassenii (catmint) is a low-growing plant with fragrant gray foliage and misty blue flowers.

The leaves of Stachys byzantina are a soft and furry silver-gray, and the plant will form mats at the front of a border.

RIGHT This sunny corner is ideal for growing a variety of foliage plants in different heights, colors, and shapes that both contrast with and complement one another.

CREATING YOUR GARDEN

2

Now you have decided on an overall plan and style for the garden, it is time to choose the plants. This section guides you through selecting the right foliage plants to create the desired effect, taking into consideration leaf size, shape, and texture. Advice is then given on how to acquire, plant, propagate, and care for foliage plants, and this is followed by a detailed discussion of the specific ways in which such plants can be used to create a whole range of fascinating features that are suitable for any garden, large or small.

LEFT *A well-balanced planting of various types of hosta and other foliage plants makes the perfect edging for this wooden path.*

LEAF SHAPE • CHOICES

ROUND LEAVES

There is a large selection of round leaves, from the almost perfectly round to those that are heart-shaped or broadly oval. The largest of all are those of *Gunnera manicata* (giant rhubarb), up to 6ft (2m) or more across. These are a feature in their own right. Moving down the scale, medium-sized and small round leaves mix well with other foliage. In some cases, as with hostas, the leaves emerge from a central point, forming a low fountain. In others they lie next to each other, often overlapping. This type of foliage has a tendency to create a horizontal accent among the hurry-skurry of other foliage. It forms an area of calm in a rough "sea", which gives the eye somewhere to rest. It contrasts well with spiky and filmy foliage.

FEATHERY LEAVES

Ferns and other feathery-leaved plants are a godsend for the foliage gardener. They exhibit a form of foliage that is extremely valuable. The shape of the leaves and fronds tends to be deeply cut, giving them a filmy quality. Ferns are the obvious example and their leaves usually form an upright fountain. *Foeniculum vulgare* (fennel), by contrast, is a tall upright plant with drooping filigree foliage. Shrubs are also represented, *Acer palmatum* 'Dissectum' being a good example, forming layers of foliage. All these different forms produce a light, airy contrast to the more solid foliage of most plants and can be used to lift a scheme. They are often light in weight as well as appearance and move nicely in a breeze.

CHOICE PLANTS CHECKLIST

- Asarum europaeum
- Astilboides tabularis
- Bergenia cordifolia
- Cyclamen coum
- Darmera peltata
- Gunnera manicata
- Hosta 'Zounds'
- Ligularia dentata
- Nymphaea
- Petasites japonicus
- Plantago major 'Rubrifolia'
- Tropaeolum majus

CHOICE PLANTS CHECKLIST

- Acer palmatum 'Dissectum'
- Adiantum venustum
- Artemisia alba 'Canescens'
- Artemisia 'Powis Castle'
- Dryopteris dilatata
- Foeniculum vulgare
- Matteuccia struthiopteris
- Onychium japonicum
- Sambucus nigra f. laciniata

SWORD-LIKE FOLIAGE

Sword-like and strap-like leaves are very similar except that sword-like leaves are usually very stiff, like those of an iris, whereas strap-like leaves, although similar in shape, tend to arch as demonstrated by *Hemerocallis* (day lily). However, both are parallel-sided leaves ending in a point and are usually quite long. Short and medium-sized plants with sword-like foliage make good contrast within a border, especially when surrounded by round leaves. However, the really big specimens such as *Phormium tenax* (New Zealand flax) or large grasses make very imposing specimen plants, either in a border or planted by themselves. Most sword-like plants make very good specimens for containers, the classic one being *Cordyline australis*.

CHOICE PLANTS CHECKLIST

- *Aciphylla aurea*
- *Cordyline australis*
- *Cortaderia selloana*
- *Crocosmia masoniorum*
- *Eryngium agavifolium*
- *Hemerocallis fulva*
- *Iris pallida* 'Variegata'
- *Miscanthus sinensis*
- *Morina longifolia*
- *Phormium tenax*
- *Typha latifolia*
- *Yucca gloriosa*

JAGGED AND DEEPLY CUT FOLIAGE

Some foliage is very dramatic, much in the same way as a rocky coastline is. The jagged leaves of *Acanthus spinosus* (bear's breeches) or the deeply cut foliage of *Cynara cardunculus* (cardoon) always stands out among the more gentle foliage of other plants. They add a touch of sudden excitement and ruffle the surface of an otherwise placid scene. However, stand back and look at them from a distance and they have the same effect as feathery foliage. They still stand out, but now seem to soften the scheme, whereas the true feathery foliage is lost by the distance. These plants look most dramatic when planted among smooth-leaved plants such as bergenia. Although not quite so dramatic, deeply cut leaves also create good contrast.

CHOICE PLANTS CHECKLIST

- *Acanthus spinosus*
- *Acer palmatum*
- *Cynara cardunculus*
- *Eryngium giganteum*
- *Fatsia japonica*
- *Macleaya cordata*
- *Mahonia japonica*
- *Melianthus major*
- *Onopordum acanthium*
- *Rheum palmatum*
- *Silybum marianum*
- *Trachycarpus fortunei*

LEAF SIZE • CHOICES

FINE LEAVES

Fine, needle-like leaves have a dual role. When seen at close range they have a delicate quality but when seen from a distance they tend to merge, forming a solid mass. A yew hedge, for example, looks very solid until you approach, when it is possible to appreciate the individual leaves. Some fine leaves such as those of fennel are almost limp, while others, such as the beautiful needles of *Pinus wallichiana*, are quite stiff in spite of their pendulous nature. What all fine leaves have in common is that they invite you to run them through your fingers; they are very tactile. Those that hang down tend to have a silky characteristic whereas those that stick out around their stem, like rosemary, appear more coarse, but this is not always the case to the touch.

CHOICE PLANTS CHECKLIST

- Abies koreana
- Bassia scoparia
  f. trichophylla
- Chamaecyparis
  lawsoniana
- Foeniculum vulgare
- Lavandula angustifolia
- Pinus wallichiana
- Ranunculus fluitans
- Rosmarinus officinalis
- Tamarix ramosissima
- Taxus baccata

SMALL LEAVES

Small leaves, unless they have some very strong characteristic, tend to be seen as a mass rather than individual leaves. They form a blanket of color, which from a distance looks quite uniform. If the leaves are shiny they may display a more uneven pattern as light is reflected in different directions. More individuality can also be achieved by using variegated forms of small-leaved plants. Small-leaved plants are good for topiary and hedges, particularly low ones. This is partly because they give a very solid finish, and partly because they are easier to trim neatly, unlike larger-leaved plants which will need to be clipped carefully to prevent the leaves being cut in half. Use small-leaved plants to create areas of calm in a boisterous border.

CHOICE PLANTS CHECKLIST

- Acaena microphylla
- Berberis thunbergii
- Betula pendula
- Buxus sempervirens
- Ceanothus impressus
- Cotoneaster horizontalis
- Euonymus fortunei
- Mentha requienii
- Nandina domestica
- Origanum vulgare
- Thymus serpyllum
- Vinca minor

 3

MEDIUM-SIZED LEAVES

The medium-sized leaves are the backbone of the foliage garden. They form the vast majority of plants, many of which do nothing more than create a pleasant background against which more distinctive foliage is displayed. There is, however, a good number of medium-leaved plants with interesting foliage. They still form more or less a background, but their varying shapes and textures can be seen individually giving the border a textured appearance. For example, the leaves of astilbe can be used to create a good broken effect. However, there are also many interesting medium-sized leaves that can be used as a feature—many of the smaller hostas, for example, or the wonderful marbled leaves of *Arum italicum* 'Marmoratum'.

CHOICE PLANTS CHECKLIST

- *Actinidia kolomikta*
- *Alchemilla mollis*
- *Arum italicum* 'Marmoratum'
- *Astilbe* x *arendsii*
- *Camellia japonica*
- *Geranium macrorrhizum*
- *Hedera helix*
- *Heuchera micrantha* var. *diversifolia* 'Palace Purple'
- *Pulmonaria saccharata*

 4

LARGE LEAVES

Large leaves are the most dramatic of all foliage types. Even those that are quite plain in outline or texture are able to catch the eye and can be used for dramatic effect. One of the biggest is *Gunnera manicata* (giant rhubarb). Such plants are best seen from a distance, perhaps used in isolation near a pond. On the other hand they can also be used in conjunction with other plants, but the planting must be on a scale that will accommodate their size. Those slightly further down the scale, such as *Rheum palmatum*, are much more easily mixed in with other foliage and, in spite of their size, can normally fit into the smaller garden as the plants do not have such a solid appearance. They make a good substitute for gunnera in the smaller garden.

CHOICE PLANTS CHECKLIST

- *Acanthus spinosus*
- *Agave americana* 'Variegata'
- *Cynara cardunculus*
- *Dicksonia antarctica*
- *Gunnera manicata*
- *Hosta sieboldiana* var. *elegans*
- *Melianthus major*
- *Musa basjoo*
- *Onopordum acanthium*
- *Rheum palmatum*

LEAF TEXTURE • CHOICES

FURRY AND VELVETY LEAVES

Furry leaves always have a fascination and there is usually a strong temptation to stroke them. For this reason they should be planted towards the front of a border where they can be reached. However, some, such as *Salvia argentea*, may suffer damage if handled too often and should be placed further back. In most cases the softness is created by hairs covering the leaves, which give the leaves a silvery appearance as well as a furry one. The furriness is not only a tactile quality, it is also a visual one— the plants appear soft and will make a good contrast to those with jagged or shiny qualities. Not all softness is due to hairs, however. The velvety texture of some hostas, for example, gives the same soft, touchable quality.

CHOICE PLANTS CHECKLIST

- Artemisia ludoviciana
- Hieracium lanatum
- Hydrangea aspera
- Lychnis coronaria
- Rhododendron lanatum
- Salix lanata
- Salvia argentea
- Salvia officinalis
- Senecio cineraria
- Stachys byzantina

GLOSSY LEAVES

Plants with glossy leaves are most welcome in a foliage garden, partly because they contrast so well with foliage of other textures and partly because they reflect light. Plant a furry *Senecio cineraria* in front of a camellia, for example, and the difference between the two will be stunning. The smoothness of glossy leaves also acts as a contrast to jagged leaves. The reflective quality of glossy leaves is very important; position them so that they catch the odd shaft of sunlight to create a delightful picture. They are also valuable when used in dark areas such as shady corners or under other plants, as they will catch odd glimmers of light and add life to what otherwise might be a dull area. Many are evergreen and will lighten the winter gloom.

CHOICE PLANTS CHECKLIST

- Arum italicum 'Marmoratum'
- Camellia japonica
- Euonymus japonicus
- Hedera helix
- Ilex aquifolium
- Maianthemum bifolium
- Nymphaea 'Froebelii'
- Ranunculus ficaria 'Brazen Hussy'
- Ricinis communis
- Rodgersia podophylla

 3

PRICKLY LEAVES

Prickly foliage has an interesting quality, partly for the sharpness of its spines and partly because of its often dramatic appearance. The spines may be a good reason to avoid it, as they can be very uncomfortable to weed near. They evolved to protect the plant against browsing animals, but can equally be used as a deterrent to prevent people entering the garden, or breaking windows close by. In some cases the prickles are an illusion and when touched the leaf is quite floppy. Both those with real and those with illusory prickles are very dramatic in appearance and can be used as high spots or contrasts when mixed with other foliage. They are particularly eye-catching on the larger plants such as the cynaras and ornopordums.

CHOICE PLANTS CHECKLIST

- *Acanthus spinosus*
- *Aciphylla aurea*
- *Argemone mexicana*
- *Cynara cardunculus*
- *Desfontainia spinosa*
- *Eryngium agavifolium*
- *Galactites tomentosa*
- *Ilex aquifolium*
- *Mahonia japonica*
- *Morina longifolia*
- *Onopordum acanthium*
- *Silybum marianum*

 4

RIBBED, PLEATED, AND PUCKERED LEAVES

Many plants have quite deep-set veins and this gives the leaf the appearance of being ribbed or pleated. *Veratrum nigrum* is a good example of this. As well as contrasting with smooth leaves, the undulations also reflect light in different directions, making a delightful interplay of light and shadow. Some are creased in more than one direction, giving them a puckered appearance a bit like seersucker. *Hosta* 'Zounds' is a good example. The variation of the surface of the leaves also has other visual benefits. For example, the pleats of alchemilla leaves often hold glistening drops of moisture that shine out like jewels. Other plants only have a single prominent central vein, which tends to fold the leaves in two so that they look like butterfly wings.

CHOICE PLANTS CHECKLIST

- *Alchemilla mollis*
- *Asplenium scolopendrium* Crispum Group
- *Crocosmia masoniorum*
- *Hedera helix*
- *Hosta* 'Zounds'
- *Plantago major* 'Rubrifolia'
- *Ricinus communis*
- *Rodgersia podophylla*
- *Veratrum nigrum*
- *Viburnum davidii*
- *Vitis coignetiae*

ACQUIRING FOLIAGE PLANTS

There are two main ways of acquiring foliage plants in the first place: either buying them or getting them from friends. Later, once you have a collection, you can increase by propagation when you need new plants. Whichever method you use, there are one or two rules to ensure that you get the best plants. Always examine them carefully and reject any you are dubious about, either because of their quality or because they are not the exact form you want. It is not wise to start off with inferior plants just because they were cheap or free. You will never be able to create a decent garden from poor plants.

Most plants are purchased from garden centers or specialist nurseries. Here the plants should be in good condition and the staff should be able to offer you advice. Other outlets, such as grocery stores which often have a few plants to sell, may seem tempting but check the plants thoroughly before you buy. Charity plant sales can be a good source of supply, but again check the plants thoroughly. Some healthy, interesting plants can be found at a good price, but poor specimens are not worthwhile.

CHECKING A PLANT

When buying a plant, look at it carefully. Reject plants that have diseases or pests. Also, any that are "drawn," so that they are tall and lanky, out of character, or starved and dwindling. You should also avoid broken or battered plants.

BELOW *To ensure that your plants will establish well and continue to produce healthy new growth, take care when buying that you select only the most suitable specimens.*

TECHNIQUE	POT-BOUND PLANTS	POINTS TO CONSIDER

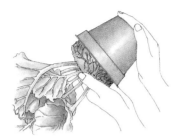

1 Before making a purchase, look carefully at the plant's roots. If they are coming out of the bottom of the pot in any quantity, carefully knock the plant out of the pot.

2 If the roots are wound around the inside of the pot in a tight mass, do not buy the plant as it may be difficult to establish; the roots may never recover.

🌢 Only buy good-quality plants. These need not be the most expensive: small nurseries are often better and cheaper than larger garden centers.
🌢 Avoid diseased plants and those covered with pests such as aphids.
🌢 Avoid pot-bound plants, where the roots have formed a tight mass around the pot.
🌢 If you buy through mail order, unpack the plants as soon as they arrive, and either plant them immediately or keep well watered.

When selecting from a group of plants of the same variety, do not automatically choose the largest plant available. Medium-sized specimens are usually the best, because the big ones tend to have a large ratio of top growth to root, and may take longer to establish than the smaller ones. On the other hand, do not buy the runts of the group either. Make sure that you only choose those plants with strong and healthy, but relatively small, new shoots.

Carefully check the roots before buying a plant. If thick roots are protruding from the bottom of the pot, gently remove the pot and examine the roots inside. If they are wound around inside the pot in a tight coil, reject the plant as the roots may continue to grow in the same fashion, even when planted in open soil.

LABELLING

Avoid plants without labels unless there is sufficient growth to show that the plant is desirable. Be cautious about labels that only give the genus: 'Hosta' for example, could mean any of several thousand varieties and may not be the color you want. It may also be an inferior plant grown from seed and there are certain types of plant that you should always see in growth before you buy. For example, *Clematis recta* 'Purpurea' is grown for its wonderful purple foliage, but many seed-grown specimens turn out to be green rather than purple, and you could get one of these if you have not seen the plant in leaf before you buy it.

MAIL ORDER

Mail order catalogues from specialist nurseries can be the only place to find many of the rarer foliage plants. They are also a good source of cultivation tips and descriptions of the plants. Nurseries may have run out of some of the plants you require, so always give alternatives or send a check or credit card number stating the upper limit you wish to pay so that it can be adjusted if all the plants are not available. Order as early as possible and let the company know when you are likely to be away. When the plants arrive, pot up immediately if necessary. Water well and place them in a shady spot for a few days to recover. Once they are growing away again they can be planted out in the normal way.

PLANTS FROM FRIENDS

One of the joys of gardening is the generosity and friendships it creates. Gardeners are constantly giving each other gifts of plants. In some cases you only have to mention that you like something and a fork appears to dig up a piece. Only accept what you really want, however. It can be a mistake to take something and then have to find a space for it in case the previous owner visits your garden in order to see it. Be careful of accepting gifts that may contain roots of weeds or pests. If you do, wash off all the soil from the roots and discard it. Then pot up the plant and grow it on for a while to check that it is healthy before you plant it out among your own plants.

INCREASING FOLIAGE PLANTS

*M**any beginners feel that propagation is a very complicated business and only those who possess "green fingers" are going to succeed. Fortunately this is a long way from the truth. The majority of plants are very easy to propagate and the more you do it the more confident you will become and your success rate will improve. Surprisingly little equipment is needed and therefore it is a cheap way of acquiring extra plants, to use yourself, to give away or to sell. When gardening on a tight budget, it is often a good idea to buy one or two plants and then propagate from these to the number you want to complete the scheme.*

There are three principal ways of increasing plants: sowing seed (bought or collected), dividing mature plants and taking cuttings. None of these is difficult to master, and it is worth learning all three of the techniques if you can.

GROWING FROM SEED

Not all plants grown from seed will be like their parents. For example, variegated plants may turn out plain green and plants with large leaves may have small ones. However, many of the naturally occuring species will "come true." Sow the seed in spring in small quantities, using a good-quality potting compost. Cover the seeds with fine grit and water well. Place the pots in a warm place out of direct sunlight, preferably in a propagator if you have one. Do not forget to label the pots. Prick out the seedlings when they are large enough to handle.

RIGHT *Most variegated plants are best propagated either by cuttings or by division.*

TECHNIQUE	DIVIDING A MATURE PLANT

1 Dig up the complete plant to be divided, taking care not to damage the roots in the process. A border fork is the best tool for this process.

2 Shake the soil from the roots. If it does not come away easily, use a hosepipe to wash it off. This will let you see what you are doing.

3 If possible, pull the plant apart into individual crowns using your fingers. For more stubborn plants, cut the crowns apart using a sharp knife.

4 Pot up the pieces into good-quality potting compost. Water and place out of the sun and wind, preferably in a cold frame, until established.

TECHNIQUE · **SOWING SEED**

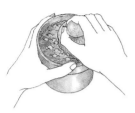 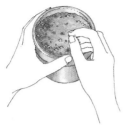 

1 Fill a pot with a good-quality seed compost and gently firm it down. A 3½in (9cm) diameter pot will usually be sufficient for a small number of seedlings.

2 Carefully sow the seed thinly on the surface of the compost, making sure that the seeds are fairly evenly spaced.

3 Cover the seed and compost with a layer of fine grit, which is usually available from garden centers. Then give each of the pots a good watering.

POINTS TO CONSIDER

🔹 Do not rely on seed-produced stock to provide identical plants to the parents as they can vary greatly.

🔹 If you are lucky, however, seed-produced plants may just turn out to be something unique, so it may be worth experimenting.

🔹 Division and cuttings produce identical offspring to the parents. They are also often faster methods than raising plants from seed.

🔹 Cuttings are ideal for propagating "sports," that is branches or shoots that are different from the main plant, and have desirable characteristics.

DIVISION

Plants created by division are identical to their parents, and this is therefore the preferred method for increasing many foliage plants with distinctive characteristics. The basic technique is to remove a part of the plant with roots on it and to replant it to form a new plant. Dig up the plant first; some seem to fall apart in your hands but others need to have the soil shaken or washed away from the roots. Then pull the plant into individual pieces, each with a growing point and some roots. If the plant does not easily come apart, cut it into sections with a sharp knife. Pot up the divisions, keep in a sheltered place and plant them out into the garden when they are established.

CUTTINGS

Cuttings will also produce plants identical to their parents and this is an ideal method for woody material and plants that are difficult to divide. Take a 4in (10cm) tip off a non-flowering shoot. Trim the shoot to 3in (7.5cm), cutting just below a leaf. Remove all the leaves except the top pair. Dip the cut end of the stem into rooting powder and then place it in cutting compost in a 3½in (9cm) pot. Up to twelve cuttings can be put in one pot, depending on the size of the leaves. Place the pot in a propagator or polythene bag until the cuttings have rooted. Pot them up and harden them off before planting out in the garden.

TECHNIQUE · **TAKING CUTTINGS**

1 Remove 4in (10cm) long shoots from a healthy plant. Choose non-flowering stems that are not too floppy nor too stiff.

2 Trim the cuttings to 3in (7.5cm), cutting through the stem just below a leaf-joint. Next remove all the leaves except the top two.

3 Place the cuttings in the compost around the edge of the pot so that the leaves of adjacent cuttings do not touch.

4 Place the pot in a propagator or polythene bag so that the leaves do not touch it. Once rooted, pot up the young plants.

PLANTING AND AFTERCARE

Before planting begins, it is important to prepare the ground thoroughly. Getting the growing conditions right to start with will save a lot of time later and may even avoid having to replace the plants if they do not thrive. After the initial enthusiasm which goes with planting, it is also important to remember that care and attention is vital, but if done properly it need be neither arduous nor time-consuming. Keep on top of things—little but often is the best approach—and try to anticipate problems before they arise.

Thorough preparation of the ground before planting is essential. If you leave pieces of weed in the soil you will be forever trying to dig them out. Prepare the ground in autumn if possible, leaving planting until spring so that any pieces of regenerating weed can be spotted and removed.

Dig over the bed, removing all weeds. Take care to remove every piece of the perennial weeds as it is no use just cutting the tops off. As you dig, incorporate as much well-rotted organic material as you can into the soil. This will not only provide nutrients for the plants but the fibrous content will help retain moisture deep in the soil where the roots of the plants need it.

As the plants are likely to be in position for many years, it pays to make a thorough job of the preparation. If the soil is heavy, this may mean double digging. This is hard work but the bed will benefit from it in the long run. Avoid bringing any subsoil to the surface and incorporate organic material in the second spade's depth as well as the upper one. If possible, leave the bed to settle for a month or two.

This allows any pieces of weed root left in the soil to start growing again and to be removed. If you plant too soon after preparation, such weeds may grow up through the desired plants and be very difficult to get out.

WEEDING

Keep the weeds under control by removing them as soon as they appear. It is much easier to pull up a few weed seedlings than to try to remove some large weed plants from between your favorite perennials. Applying a mulch to the soil surface will greatly reduce the number of new weeds germinating. Try to use an organic mulch, such as leafmould, chipped bark, or grass cuttings.

SUPPORTING

Many plants need support, especially if the site is a windy one. Do this in plenty of time, as it is very difficult to support a plant that has already collapsed. Newly planted trees and tall shrubs should be supported with stakes and

TECHNIQUE **MULCHING**

1 Weed the ground thoroughly before applying a mulch, and also water the soil first in dry weather.

2 Lay the mulch between the plants, taking care not to bury the leaves. Aim for a layer about 4in (10cm) thick.

3 Check the border every few months and top up any bare patches that appear using fresh mulch.

TECHNIQUE — STAKING WITH PEA STICKS

1 Push pea sticks (twiggy branches) into the ground in a circle around the plant you want to support, allowing for a degree of spread.

2 Bend over the tops of the sticks and tie them together to create a mesh through which the plant will grow, keeping it upright and well shaped.

TECHNIQUE — CANES AND STRING

1 Insert a number of bamboo canes into the soil around and in the middle of the plant you wish to stake.

2 Weave a cat's cradle of string around the sticks to create a mesh through which the plant shoots will grow.

POINTS TO CONSIDER

🌿 Always prepare the ground thoroughly before planting.

🌿 Mulch the soil between the plants after planting to retain moisture in the soil and prevent weeds germinating. An organic mulch is preferable.

🌿 Try to anticipate problems before they arise. For example, stake plants early rather than waiting for them to collapse.

🌿 Keep on top of the maintenance—little and often is a good regime to follow.

🌿 An hour's weeding and mulching in early spring will save many hours of work later on in the year. Prevention is always better than cure.

ABOVE *Some plants always need supporting, whether they are grown in the border or in containers. For a natural look, use the long slender twigs that are known as pea sticks.*

proper tree ties. Taller herbaceous plants can be supported in a number of ways. These include pushing twiggy branches into the ground around the plant, or using some of the wide selection of proprietary supports available.

WATERING AND FEEDING

If plenty of organic material was dug into the soil at the time of preparing the bed, and the soil has been covered with a mulch, there should be little need to water except in cases of extreme drought. If dry soil is a continuing problem, then choose plants that prefer dry conditions. Try to top-dress the borders with an organic mulch such as garden compost or farmyard manure at least once every year. This should provide enough nutrients. If unavailable, use a general fertilizer in spring, but do not overfeed.

KEEPING TIDY

Keep the borders tidy and remove dead material as it occurs. Make certain that the winter clear-up is done before the plants start back into growth in spring, as the newly emerging shoots are easily damaged.

BOLD FOLIAGE AS FOCAL POINTS

Plants with bold foliage are undoubtedly the stars of the garden. They are usually very dramatic and have a tendency to draw the eye. This makes them ideal for creating focal points within the garden. They may be in isolation, say, at the end of a lawn or at the end of a path, or even among other plants in a border, as long as they are strong enough to stand out. Bold foliage usually refers to size, but it can also refer to color. For example, a brightly variegated plant could be used as a focal point against a backdrop of plain green.

One of the best examples of bold foliage is *Gunnera manicata* (giant rhubarb), which is best displayed in isolation or in a position where it stands out from its surroundings. This does tend to mean that there is only room for it in a large garden. (However, one famous gardener grew it in a small front garden to great effect.) It grows particularly well in damp positions, such as next to a pond or stream,

where it also looks particularly good, especially when seen across water. Wherever it is planted, remember that it can grow very large, up to 15ft (4.5m) across, so allow plenty of space. Giant rhubarb is slightly tender and consequently it needs to have some frost protection in winter. One way to provide this is to cover the crown of the plant with its own dead or dying leaves to protect it.

TECHNIQUE	PLANTING GIANT RHUBARB	STAR PLANTS

STAR PLANTS

- *Acanthus spinosus*
- *Cordyline australis*
- *Cortaderia selloana*
- *Fatsia japonica* 'Variegata'
- *Gunnera manicata*
- *Miscanthus sinensis*
- *Musa basjoo*
- *Onopordum acanthium*
- *Phormium tenax*
- *Rheum palmatum*
- *Trachycarpus fortunei*
- *Yucca gloriosa*

1 Try to position the giant rhubarb on the far side of a pond where it can be seen across the water. It can be surrounded by other vegetation, but looks best on its own.

2 Dig a large hole and fork plenty of well-rotted organic material into the bottom, such as farmyard manure or leaf mold. This will help retain moisture.

3 Plant the giant rhubarb so that the top of the root ball is level with the surface of the soil. Backfill the hole and firm down.

4 Top-dress the soil with a 4in (10cm) layer of mulch such as leaf mold or weed-free farmyard manure.

5 In winter, cover the exposed crowns of the plant with its own dead leaves or with a thick layer of bracken or straw.

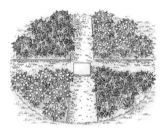

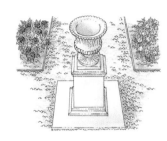

1 Any place where two paths cross makes an ideal situation for a focal point. A rose garden, herb garden, or a bed of annuals will be improved with a dramatic centerpiece.

2 To make a really dramatic focal point, stand the container on a plinth. Be sure to place the plinth and the pot in position before planting begins.

3 Place some broken tiles or small stones in the bottom of the pot to help with the drainage. Make sure you cover the drainage holes to hold the compost in place.

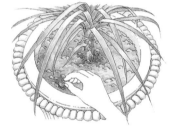

4 Fill the pot with a good-quality potting compost and firm it down gently. It is advisable to use a soil-based compost for permanent plantings, as this will retain moisture better.

5 Plant the feature plant (here a cordyline), firm it down and adjust the level of the compost so that the surface is about 1in (3cm) below the rim of the pot.

6 Place a plug of slow-release fertilizer just below the surface of the compost. This will provide the necessary nutrients for the plant over several months. Water the container throughly.

LEFT *A selection of different colored grasses grown in eye-catching containers makes a spectacular patio display.*

USING CONTAINERS

Focal points do not always have to be in isolation; often they will be a centerpiece of a border or series of borders. For example, one may have a large circular rose garden with one or more paths crossing it. In the center, where the paths meet, it is usually a good idea to have a feature such as a large urn on a plinth with a striking plant in it. One of the most suitable plants is *Cordyline australis* with its neatly arrayed sword-like leaves. The symmetrical nature of the plant makes it perfect for a formal position.

Such a container will be heavy to move so it is best to position it before adding the plant and compost.

USING TOPIARY

opiary has been a feature of gardens for many centuries and its popularity is set to continue. It is easier than ever to create, since it is now possible to buy a wide range of "formers" from garden centers. These frames allow the gardener to fashion any number of topiary shapes, from simple geometric balls and pyramids to more complicated figures such as sheep and peacocks. Topiary is not difficult; it just requires a steady hand and plenty of patience, because the best shrubs to use also tend to be the slowest-growing.

The best plants to use for topiary are those with small, densely packed leaves. These will achieve a neater shape and you can trim them with shears without cutting the individual leaves in half which will make the topiary look unsightly. Also, try to choose slow-growing plants to avoid the need for constant clipping. The speed of growth can be frustrating while you are waiting for the topiary to assume its shape, but once it has the slow growth means that it will keep its shape. A quick-growing plant will soon become overgrown and need regular pruning. *Buxus sempervirens* (box) and *Taxus baccata* (yew) are the best.

A MOP-HEADED BAY TREE

The classic position for mop-headed bay trees is on either side of a doorway, although they can be used in many other positions. Indeed, they can also be used in any quantity, from a single specimen to a number of plants spread evenly down either side of a path, for example, to set up a marvelous rhythm. Patience is required as the bay will take several years to get to the required height, but this can be shortened by buying a mature plant. Pruning such a plant is best done with secateurs rather than shears as it is important not to cut the leaves in half or they will look dreadful.

PROJECT	CREATING A MOP-HEADED BAY TREE	STAR PLANTS

1 Plant a young bay tree in a pot, putting small stones in the bottom and using a good-quality potting compost.

2 As the plant grows, remove any new shoots that arise from the base and allow the main stem to grow straight.

3 Trim off any sideshoots that appear back to just two buds or leaves, making certain to use a pair of sharp secateurs.

4 When the plant reaches its final height, allow the top to bush out. Remove all the lower sideshoots flush with the stem.

5 As the top fills out, clip it regularly so that it becomes shaped like a ball. Prune twice a year to keep it neat.

6 Foliage makes a good foil to the straight lines of an entrance door. These neat bay bushes create a formal effect.

STAR PLANTS

- *Buxus sempervirens* (box)
- *Hedera colchica* (Persian ivy)
- *Hedera helix* (common ivy)
- *Ilex aquifolium* (holly)
- *Laurus nobilis* (bay laurel)
- *Ligustrum ovalifolium* 'Aureum' (golden privet)
- *Lonicera nitida* 'Baggesen's Gold' (poor man's box)
- *Taxus baccata* Aureus Group (golden yew)

PROJECT **QUICK IVY TOPIARY**

1 Choose a topiary former from a garden center or nursery and cover it with a fine-meshed wire netting. This will ensure even coverage of the ivy foliage.

2 Place the former either in the ground or in a container. The ground is a better choice as the plant will require less attention, especially watering and feeding.

3 Plant one or more ivy plants around the base of the former, ensuring that the tops of the root balls are level with the surface of the soil or compost.

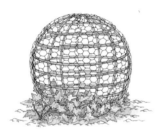

4 Train the stems of the ivy around the base of the former. As it grows, continue to train the foliage round the base until it is completely encircled.

5 The ivy will now grow up and over the former until it is completely covered. Tuck in any wayward shoots that stick out and direct them to empty areas.

6 Clip over the ivy every so often to ensure that it is kept neat and grows tight against the former to maintain an accurate and tidy shape.

LEFT *In an informal setting, clipped shapes need not be so tightly defined—but the overall outline should still be clear.*

QUICK TOPIARY

On the whole, topiary shapes are best made from slow-growing shrubs such as box or yew, partly because they have dense foliage and partly because they hold their shape and do not require frequent clipping. However, they do take a long time to mature. One way of beating the clock is to use *Hedera helix* (ivy) instead, which can be trained over a metal former and will make a very quick, neat topiary. Other climbers can be used but they are more difficult to control, whereas ivy can be kept compact. Any variety can be used, even a variegated one, but a small-leaved ivy looks best as it is neater and more compact.

WATER AND FOLIAGE

ater and foliage were made for each other. Both create a sense of serenity and tranquillity that is very difficult to better in a garden. The foliage complements the water in a number of ways. It softens the edge of a pond, creating a sense of mystery as the surface of the water disappears beneath it. It breaks up the surface, preventing it from becoming too boring, and it picks up the reflections that come from the water. It also has a more practical purpose, in that plants provide the water with oxygen which is essential for pond life. Without plants, stagnant water can become smelly and unpleasant.

Water and waterside plants can be divided into three groups. Within the water itself there are the submerged plants, such as the oxygenating plants, many of which have fascinating foliage, some hair-like and dainty, others forming tight cylinders. Other aquatic plants include more decorative subjects that float on the surface, including *Nymphaea* (water lilies). Next are the marginal plants that will live in shallow water around the edges of a pond. Many of these are grown for their foliage effect, including *Typha*, the upright reed maces. Others, however, including the stately *Iris laevigata,* are also appreciated for their flowers. The third group of plants consists of those that prefer to inhabit the boggy soil or the banks around the pond. These can include any plants that like moist conditions, such as *Rodgersia podophylla* and many of the very beautiful filigree ferns such as *Osmunda regalis* (royal fern) and *Matteuccia struthiopteris* (shuttlecock fern).

MAKING A HALF-BARREL POND

Not all gardens have space for a pond, but it is still possible, even in the smallest patio garden, to make room for a water feature to add a cooling influence to the scene and provide a water source for birds and insects. One good idea for a small-scale water feature is a barrel pond, made from half a wooden barrel which can sit on any paved area, or even in a border. The barrel, obviously, must be suitable for a pond, that is it must be watertight. There is not going to be much room in a half-barrel for many plants, especially as it essential that not all the surface area is covered; some water must be left showing. The best plant combination is to have an upright plant, such as *Iris laevigata* 'Variegata' with its handsome stripy foliage that rises through the water surface, and a floating leaf such as a small water lily (*Nymphaea* 'Aurora', for example) as a contrast. Position the half-barrel pond in full sun.

TECHNIQUE **PLANTING AN AQUATIC PLANT IN A POND**

1 Plant water plants in lattice pots that have been lined with hessian to prevent the compost from falling out. Use a special aquatic compost.

2 Thread two long strings through either side of the pot so it can be suspended across the middle of the pond.

3 With one person on either side of the pond, lower the basket very carefully into the water between you so that it finishes in the required position.

4 One person then gradually releases the strings and the other gently pulls them free of the pot and out of the pond, leaving the pot in position.

STAR PLANTS

- *Acorus calamus* 'Variegatus' (sweet flag)
- *Iris laevigata* 'Variegata'
- *Matteuccia struthiopteris* (shuttlecock fern)
- *Nymphaea* (water lilies)
- *Onoclea sensibilis* (sensitive fern)
- *Osmunda regalis* (royal fern)
- *Ranunculus fluitans* (water buttercup)
- *Rodgersia podophylla*
- *Thelypteris palustris* (marsh fern)
- *Typha latifolia* (reed mace)

1 Drape the inside of a half-barrel with hessian sacking and soak it with water. This will cause the staves of the barrel to swell and become watertight.

2 When the wood has swollen up sufficiently to hold water, place the barrel in position and fill it up using a hosepipe or watering can.

3 Line a lattice pot with hessian and fill with aquatic compost. Put the plant into the compost and firm down. Repeat this with all the plants you are using.

4 Carefully lower the pots into the water, taking care to position them at the right depth. Stand them on bricks or empty flower pots, if necessary.

5 Top up the water level to about 1in (3cm) below the rim. Check the water level regularly; if it drops too much, the staves may shrink, causing the barrel to leak.

LEFT *"Water plants" include those that grow in deep water with their leaves floating on the surface, such as* Nymphaea *(water lilies), and the marginal plants that like to have their roots in the damp soil found around the edges of the pool.*

PLANTING A LARGER POND

A larger pond can be planted in a similar way, being careful to balance the various elements so that the pond does not become overcrowded. A larger pond may have a varied depth, making it possible to grow plants that like deep water, and marginals that like shallow water. Deep-water plants include submerged plants that provide oxygen. These are often attractive as well as practical. Most plants that grow on or above the surface of the water, such as water lilies, also have flowers although almost all are valuable as foliage plants in their own right.

FOLIAGE AS A FOIL

As well as being interesting in its own right, foliage also acts beautifully as a foil for setting off other garden features. These may be other plants, especially flowering plants or plants with particularly striking foliage effects, or they may be man-made objects such as statues or other pieces of sculpture. The foil can be just a bland background of greenery, but usually it is much more interesting if it is structured in such a way so as to enhance the feature. With some statues, classical pieces perhaps, the background needs to be formal, whereas with others a more informal romantic setting may be required.

Formal sculptures often do best in a formal setting and such a setting should have a uniform background. Often a hedge, such as *Taxus baccata* (yew), makes the perfect backdrop as it is uniform in both color and texture and has a particularly formal effect when clipped. The dark color of the leaves sets off the pale tones of stone or metals. Statues can be set in front of such a hedge or they can be set into them. A neat niche can be carved into an existing hedge, or created in a new hedge, so that the hedge appears to wrap around the sculpture.

Another way to set off a statue is to position it against a hedge or wall and then flank it with two mop-headed bay trees (*Laurus nobilis*) in containers. In a formal position, sculpture should always sit on a plinth.

INFORMAL SETTINGS

Many pieces of sculpture lend themselves to an informal setting. Here the sculpture can almost be enveloped by the soft, abundant greenery around it. Indeed, with many romantic settings, the sculpture is so embraced that it seems as if it is peering out of the undergrowth. In other situations it needs no more than a few trails of ivy or the careful positioning of a fern to set the work off. In informal settings, sculptures are often shown to best advantage on the ground; there is no need to bring them up to eye level.

BELOW *This formal herb garden has a stone ornament as a focal point. It is perfectly framed by the dark, shaped hedge behind it, and the narrow grass paths forming a cross at its base.*

| PROJECT | FORMAL SCULPTURE | STAR PLANTS |

 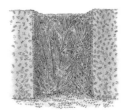 

1 A sculpture is best set on a plinth against a tightly clipped dark yew hedge. Place one or more paving slabs under the plinth if it is standing on grass, to facilitate mowing around the base.

2 It is possible to cut out a section of an existing yew hedge to create a niche in which to place a sculpture. It will take several years for the foliage to grow back around the inside of the niche.

3 If planting a new hedge with niches, make sure that the hedge is thick by using a double row of shrubs. Omit one or more shrubs on one side of the hedge to form the niche.

STAR PLANTS

- *Buxus sempervirens* (box)
- *Dryopteris dilatata* (broad buckler fern)
- *Fagus sylvatica* 'Riversii' (copper beech)
- *Hedera helix* (common ivy)
- *Hosta sieboldiana* var. *elegans*
- *Humulus lupulus* 'Aureus' (golden hop)
- *Laurus nobilis* (bay laurel)
- *Taxus baccata* (yew)
- *Vitis vinifera* 'Purpurea' (purple-leaved grape)

4 To create a very formal effect in a gravel garden, place a piece of sculpture in front of a dark hedge and flank it with two bay trees that have been clipped as mop-heads.

5 Formal sculpture looks good when placed against foliage at the end of a long path or vista. Here a tall plinth has been used to make a clear focal point.

6 Even sculpture in a formal position can be enhanced by a small amount of informal foliage near or around the plinth. Hostas and *Hedera helix* (ivy) are ideal for this situation.

| PROJECT | INFORMAL SCULPTURE |

1 Set a piece of sculpture in a foliage border so that it peeps out from among the leaves. Do not let it get completely swamped by the growing foliage, however.

2 In a formal setting, the sculpture can be given a more casual and informal appearance simply by growing ivy around or over it. Trim the ivy regularly to keep it in check.

3 A single fern and a trailing vine such as *Vitis vinifera* 'Purpurea' can make a piece of sculpture look informal. Make sure they do not grow over it and obscure it completely.

4 Make a new piece of sculpture look older and more informal by brushing it over with sour milk so that lichen and algae becomes quickly established.

FRAGRANT FOLIAGE

Fragrance is not used in the garden as much as it should be. Nearly all foliage has some fragrance when crushed, the majority no more than a "green" smell, but a large number have a wonderful aroma, whether it is a sharp citrus tang or a heady mellow scent. Some plants emit the scent spontaneously, but others have to be crushed or at least brushed before the fragrance becomes apparent. Scented foliage should be placed near a path or the edge of a lawn so that you can run your fingers through it as you pass. A whole path lined with lavender or rosemary is a joy to walk through. Plant seats can also be created.

The idea of plant seats can be traced back to medieval times and even beyond. Chamomile is the most popular choice because it is tough but also fragrant, so that the sitters are wreathed in scent. The seat can be made from wood, but bricks last longer (*see technique below*). The best chamomile is *Chamaemelum nobile* 'Treneague' as it is low-growing and does not flower. Trim it over if it gets a bit too long. *Thymus* (thyme) may be used as an alternative.

A LAVENDER PATH

A lavender path is easy to create yet gives an abundance of pleasure. The lavender should overhang the path so that you can brush against it to release the scent and trail fingers through it. It has flowers in summer which are also highly perfumed, but the foliage is present all year round. It is cheap to create as you can buy one plant and take cuttings from it, then use the resulting plants to create the path.

PROJECT | **MAKING A CHAMOMILE SEAT**

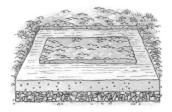

1 Dig the foundations 8in (20cm) wide and 10in (25cm) deep. Fill the hole first with 4in (10cm) of rammed hardcore and then with 4in (10cm) of concrete.

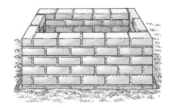

2 When the concrete for the foundations has set firmly, build a brick wall on top, to a height of 16–20in (40–50cm) above soil level. Allow the mortar to set.

STAR PLANTS

- *Acorus calamus* 'Variegatus'
- *Aloysia triphylla*
- *Chamaemelum nobile* 'Treneague'
- *Geranium macrorrhizum*
- *Laurus nobilis*
- *Lavandula angustifolia*
- *Rosmarinus officinalis*
- *Salvia officinalis*
- *Santolina chamaecyparissus*
- *Tanacetum parthenium* 'Aureum'
- *Thymus serpyllum*

3 Nail a wooden surround around the top of the brickwork, with a chamfered edge to make the seat more comfortable.

4 Fill the seat with soil and allow it to settle through the winter. Top up with more soil in spring to the level of the rim.

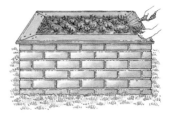

5 Plant the chamomile plants at 6in (15cm) intervals across the surface of the compost and water them in well.

PLANTING A LAVENDER PATH

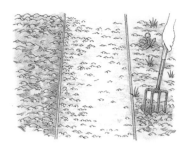 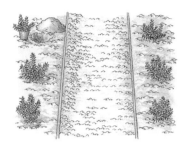 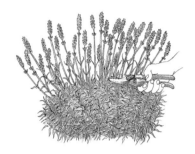

1 First prepare the soil on either side of the path thoroughly. Dig it over carefully with a fork, removing all the weeds, and then work in some well-rotted organic material. Finally, level the surface of the soil using a flat-headed rake.

2 Carefully position the lavender plants down either side of the path, making sure that you plant them to the same depth they were in their pots. Space the plants 24in (60cm) apart and about 10in (25cm) in from the edge of the path.

3 Remove the dead flower heads from the plants when they begin to fade, using secateurs or shears. In spring, trim over the previous year's foliage growth to neaten the appearance of the plants before they start to flower.

A THYME PATH

Thyme is tough enough to withstand being trodden on so it makes a wonderful, fragrant addition to a path. When lightly crushed, it releases a delicious scent, reminiscent of chalk downlands. Position a few plants along a path or walkway, but avoid areas where elderly people may trip over them. Plant in the cracks between paving slabs or bricks. Alternatively, lift a brick or slab and plant the whole area with thyme. Clip the plants over in spring.

PROJECT   MAKING A THYME PATH

1 Use a masonry trowel to scrape out the cement between two bricks or slabs, right down to the loose sand or earth below it.

2 Lower a rooted thyme cutting into the gap and fill the space around its roots with a fine potting compost. Water well and keep moist.

ABOVE *A path surrounded by thyme will be fragrant all year round, when footsteps brush the scented foliage, but it also looks stunning when the plants are in full summer flower.*

SOUND AND FOLIAGE

Sound is nearly as important in the garden as aspects that appeal to any of the other senses. The tinkling of water and the rustling of leaves help to provide a restful atmosphere that is vital in any outside space. The dead leaves of beech hedges or grasses in winter provide a pleasing rustle, as do the green leaves of bamboo or ornamental grasses in summer. One of the stranger noises, however, is the rubbing together of the prickly stems of the giant rhubarb; in a breeze it sounds like a giant rubbing the designer stubble on his chin. Yet not all sound is welcome, especially that coming from outside the garden.

Bamboo is one of the best plants to choose for creating a pleasant sound. Even the lightest breeze will set off a gentle rustle. Remember to choose a non-invasive form, unless you have a garden big enough to accommodate a very large clump. If you are in doubt about the one you have bought, surround the roots with a sheet of metal or plastic so that they cannot spread too far. Such contained plants, however, can eventually become very congested and will have to be dug up and divided from time to time. Rejuvenate the soil before replanting a young, healthy portion with roots. A few bamboos flower and may die out after flowering, but the majority only flower very occasionally.

TECHNIQUE	PLANTING BAMBOO

1 Prepare the ground in the autumn, removing any perennial weeds and incorporating plenty of well-rotted organic material into the soil.

2 In the following spring, rake through the bed and carefully remove any pieces of weed that have regenerated or germinated since the autumn.

3 Dig the planting hole and set the bamboo in it so that the top of the root ball is level with the surface of the soil. Fill in around the roots and firm down. Water the plant carefully.

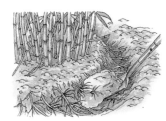

4 If the bamboo proves to be over-vigorous, dig a trench around the clump and prune back the roots using secateurs. This can be done every year.

5 Alternatively, insert a tough barrier, such as a sheet of metal, in the trench around the bamboo. Rigid plastic will also do, but polythene sheets are likely to be too flimsy.

STAR PLANTS

- *Arundo donax* (giant reed)
- *Bambusa multiplex* (hedge bamboo)
- *Chusquea culeou*
- *Cortaderia selloana* (pampas grass)
- *Fagus sylvatica* (beech)
- *Gunnera manicata* (giant rhubarb)
- *Miscanthus sinensis* (eulalia)
- *Phyllostachys nigra* (black bamboo)
- *Sasa veitchii* (kuma zasa)

CUTTING OUT SOUND

Unfortunately it is not always possible to be totally cut off from the outside world, however private the garden. Sounds from roads or neighbors can still filter in. By planting a rustling bamboo or grass you start to drown out the noise with your own, more pleasurable one, but outside noise will still be present, especially on still days.

One way, at least, of blocking some of the outside noise is to plant a thick hedge around the boundary. Even more sound will be deadened if there are plenty of other trees and shrubs in the garden to absorb it. The hedge should be evergreen, such as *Taxus baccata* (yew) or *Ilex aquifolium* (holly). If there is space, use a double row of shrubs for maximum noise absorption.

To help reduce sound further, it is a good idea to plant extra shrubs around areas where you sit and relax. Creating a dense arbor with a sitting area right in its heart is very comforting and really keeps you away from the noisy world outside. Such features take time to grow, but do not be tempted to use fast-growing plants. Although they will reach the required size quickly, they will continue to grow and may need constant pruning thereafter.

RIGHT *A bamboo screen can serve a dual purpose in the garden: it helps to cushion unwanted outside noises, and in a breeze it creates its own, more relaxing, rustling sounds.*

TECHNIQUE	PLANTING A NOISE-ABSORBING YEW HEDGE

1 Dig over the soil along the line of the hedge, removing all perennial weeds and adding as much well-rotted organic material as you can lay your hands on.

2 Using a string line for guidance, plant two parallel rows of yew plants, 12in (30cm) apart, at 24in (60cm) intervals. Stagger the plants in the rows.

3 As soon as individual branches reach the height and spread that you require, trim them back. Eventually the whole hedge will fill out to the required shape.

THE HOT AND DRY FOLIAGE GARDEN

Foliage plants can be used to enhance hot, dry areas as much as the shady, damp parts of the garden. Plants in shade often grow lush and green to make the most of the available light, but those that have evolved in hot, dry areas often need some protection from the sun and may grow silvery hairs to reflect sunlight and keep the leaves cool. Many silver-leaved plants make handsome additions to the hot, dry garden and create a Mediterranean feel. There are also others, such as the purple-leaved plants and many of the leathery-leaved plants, that also need sun and can be used to provide a contrast of color and texture.

The main problem with hot, dry areas is the dry element. Many plants that prefer the shade can be grown in sun if they are given plenty of moisture. Hostas, for example, will grow very happily in the open given a moist soil. However, for hot and dry soil you will need plants that naturally grow in these conditions. On the whole, this will mean plants that have their origins in Mediterranean areas. Not all Mediterranean plants are suitable, though, because they will have to withstand a cold winter, or worse still wet winter weather. A combination of cold and damp will cause many such plants to rot and die.

Many of the plants suitable for hot, dry areas are those with deep tap roots, such as *Eryngium* (sea hollies). Such plants are capable of sending their roots well down into the soil to look for moisture. These plants also tend to have small leaves, to limit the surface area and hence the amount of moisture lost through them.

ADAPTING HEAVY SOILS

Heavy soils are likely to be wetter than light soils, especially in winter. Nevertheless, it is still possible to create a Mediterranean-style bed in these conditions. There are two methods of achieving this. The first is to add plenty of gravel to the existing soil in order to lighten it and make it more free-draining. The second method is to ignore the soil altogether and build a raised bed above it.

CREATING A RAISED BED

Raised beds are useful features in that you can control the conditions within them, and if desired use a different soil type to the rest of the garden. For growing Mediterranean-style plants, fill the bed with a light, free-draining soil that will not become over-wet in winter. Raised beds can be

created from various materials, such as bricks or stones, but railroad ties are an attractive option if you can get hold of them. See the technique below for instructions on how to make a raised bed with railroad ties.

PROJECT	A RAISED BED

1 In autumn, thoroughly dig over the soil beneath the area for the raised bed, and incorporate plenty of grit, gravel or sharp sand, as well as the usual organic material.

2 Make a raised bed on the dug-over soil, using railroad ties to form the sides. The bed can be any shape or size, but it is best to make it so that you can reach into the middle.

3 When the framework of ties is complete, fill the bed with a good free-draining loam, preferably one that has plenty of sand in it.

4 Firm down the soil and plant up the bed with your chosen plants. Water them in well, then top-dress the soil with gravel, to suppress weed growth.

STAR PLANTS

- *Acaena saccaticupula* 'Blue Haze'
- *Agave americana* 'Variegata' (century plant)
- *Convolvulus cneorum*
- *Cordyline australis*
- *Eryngium variifolium* (variegated sea holly)
- *Euphorbia characias* subsp. *wulfenii* (Mediterranean spurge)
- *Lavandula angustifolia* (lavender)
- *Onopordum acanthium* (Scotch thistle)
- *Rosmarinus officinalis* (rosemary)
- *Salvia officinalis* 'Purpurascens' (purple sage)
- *Stachys byzantina* (lamb's ears)

A DRY RIVER BED

A more ornamental feature can be created by landscaping the area to form a winding dry river bed with raised banks. The dry river bed can include rounded stones of various sizes and pieces of weather-worn wood. Plant the banks with grasses and Mediterranean-style plants to enhance the effect, and add a few plants to the river bed itself. The bed will look most natural if it is built on naturally undulating ground, but the area can be artificially landscaped to good effect. Choose a mixture of plants, including a few spiky grasses, some hummock-forming thymes or sages and a few carpeting plants, such as *Acaena saccaticupula* 'Blue Haze'. Plant fairly sparsely to make it look more natural.

ABOVE *Plants such as these cacti and succulents have adapted naturally to living in* *very dry areas, and even in deserts. This can be used to advantage in hot, dry sites.*

PROJECT   **MAKING A DRY RIVER BED**

1 Excavate a slightly winding, shallow depression in an area of light soil. Pile the soil up on either side of the hollow and smooth it to create a gentle hump.

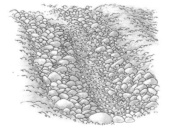

2 Cover the depressed area with gravel, and then randomly add smooth rounded stones of varying sizes in order to give the impression of a dried-up river bed.

3 Plant a selection of grasses and other drought-tolerant plants, such as thymes and sages, along the banks, with a few placed in the river bed itself.

FOLIAGE FOR DAMP SOIL

Some of the finest of foliage plants thrive in the lush conditions supplied by damp ground. Many of these plants have large or dramatic leaves and, because of the moisture, they stay looking fresh and vibrant all summer long. If you do not have an area of damp soil in the garden, it is easy to create a bog garden which will let you take advantage of these stunning plants. Few will survive in completely waterlogged conditions, but there are plenty of plants that will enjoy a certain amount of moisture around their roots.

In gardens where you do not want to create a bog garden, it is possible to create a simple moisture-retentive bed to grow a large number of plants that like damp but not boggy conditions. Here it will be sufficient to incorporate plenty of leaf mold or other well-rotted organic material into the soil. This will hold moisture down by the plants' roots to allow them to thrive without too much watering. A good mulch of at least 4in (10cm) of organic material will also help. Avoid making such a bed near trees or a hedge as the roots will soon extract the moisture from the soil.

BOG GARDENS

Few gardens have soil sufficiently moist to make a natural bog garden. However, it is not to difficult to create an artificial one; the secret is to use a pond liner to help hold the moisture. Unlike a pond, however, the liner is punctured at its lowest points to allow excess moisture to drain away, leaving the soil damp rather than waterlogged. Any type of pond liner will do; even thick polythene can be used as no light can reach it to degrade it. The bog garden is filled with a fibrous soil, rich in organic matter, which itself will also hold moisture. The moisture level is kept topped up by using a drip or seep hose buried in the soil. This can be connected to the mains water supply and turned on when required or, better still, connected to a water barrel that collects rainwater. If the bog garden is created next to a pond, the pond can be designed to overflow into the bog garden in times of excess rainfall.

PLANTING A BOG GARDEN

A wide range of plants can be used to plant a bog garden. It is best to use those plants that are used to growing in water on the margins of ponds—tall irises for example, towards the center where the soil is likely to be at its most moist. Use plants that like less moisture, such as hostas, towards the sides of the bog garden.

STAR PLANTS

- *Adiantum venustum*
- *Aruncus dioicus*
- *Blechnum spicant*
- *Darmera peltata*
- *Gunnera manicata*
- *Iris laevigata*
- *Ligularia dentata* 'Desdemona'
- *Lobelia* 'Queen Victoria'
- *Matteuccia struthiopteris*
- *Onoclea sensibilis*
- *Osmunda regalis*
- *Persicaria bistorta*
- *Rodgersia podophylla*
- *Thelypteris palustris*

PROJECT	A PONDSIDE BOG GARDEN

1 Dig a bog garden in the same way as described on the next page, but position it close to a pond, leaving a narrow ridge of high ground between the bog garden and the pond.

2 Lower the ridge until it is just above the proposed water level of the pond. Line the bog garden and then the pond, bringing the pond's liner over the ridge into the bog garden.

3 Fill the bog garden with soil up to the level of the ridge, but do not include a perforated pipe as you would in a free-standing bog garden. Plant the bog garden with moisture-loving plants.

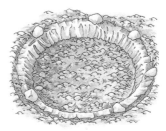

1 Dig out a shallow hole about 12–18in (30–45cm) deep and as large as you want the bog garden to be. Then line the hole with either a pond liner or thick polythene.

2 Make a few holes in the liner at its lowest points using a garden fork. Place a series of large stones or bricks around the edges of the liner to hold it in place.

3 Part-fill the liner with a good-quality loam that has been mixed with equal parts of leaf mold, or another organic material such as well-rotted garden compost.

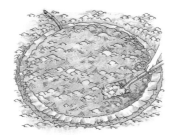

4 Lay a perforated pipe or drip hose across the surface of the soil so that it is evenly distributed over the bog garden. A spiral arrangement is best in a circular bed.

5 Continue to fill the bed with the soil mixture until you have filled the depression. Leave the soil slightly heaped up to allow for the soil to sink.

6 Lay paving slabs at intervals across the bed to make stepping stones to give access to the whole bed without standing directly in the soil. Plant up the bog garden.

A BOG GARDEN NEXT TO A POND

A similar bog garden can be created next to a pond, except that the pond's liner is continued from the pond over a ledge just above water level into the bog garden. When the water level of the pond rises during heavy rain, the excess water flows over the ledge into the bog garden where it soaks the soil. The excess water then seeps out of the bottom of the bog garden into the soil below. During very dry weather, it may be necessary to top up the pond using a hosepipe. If you have to do this, allow the hose to run until the pond overflows into the bog garden.

LEFT *A bog garden makes the perfect companion for a natural-looking pond. It also enables the gardener to grow an even greater range of plants. Many of those that like to have their roots in permanently moist soil have striking, lush foliage.*

FOLIAGE FOR VERTICAL SPACES

Every garden should be thought of as a three-dimensional space. This is partly a visual approach to the garden and partly due to the desire of most gardeners to use every scrap of room to grow as many plants as they can. A lot of climbers are grown for their flowers— roses, for example—but there are some that are grown either for their foliage alone, such as Parthenocissus henryana *(Chinese Virginia creeper), or for their foliage and their flowers, such as* Hydrangea anomala subsp. petiolaris, *for example. Such climbers can be used to grow up walls or other structures, or to hang down in attractive swags, like creepers.*

Climbers can be used in two different ways. The first is purely aesthetic, perhaps to create a leafy background or provide a vertical accent to a border. The second is more functional, for example to clad an unslightly wall or shed, to cover a pergola or to soften a harsh shape. Choose the type of climber that is most suited to the job. *Hedera* (ivy), is self-supporting, while *Humulus* (hops) twine around their host, and plants such as clematis cling on with tendrils.

PLANTING CLIMBERS

The main foliage climbers (*Hedera* and *Parthenocissus*) are self-supporting and need no help when they are planted next to walls, fences, or trees. However, they do need to

RIGHT *The bright red autumn foliage of* Parthenocissus *(Virginia creeper) contrasts beautifully with the yellow-variegated forms of* Hedera *(ivy), creating a vertical feast.*

TECHNIQUE	PLANTING A CLIMBER CLOSE TO A WALL

1 Dig a hole at least 12in (30cm) from the wall (it must not be too close to the wall), and dig plenty of well-rotted compost or farmyard manure into it.

2 Place the plant in the hole and make sure that the top of the root ball is level with the soil surface. Fill in the hole and firm down. Water well.

3 Use canes angled from the base of the plant to the wall to train the shoots to grow in the right direction. You will also need to attach some canes to the wall.

be planted properly to get them off to a good start. The main problem is the dry soil that is nearly always found close to walls. To counter this, the soil should be enriched and the climber set a little distance from the wall, with its shoots trained on canes to reach the wall.

CLIMBER CURTAINS

There is a naturally tendency to think of climbers as climbing up, but they can also be used to hang down. They can be trained to hang over horizontal structures, such as fences, walls, or balustrades, to create swags of hanging vegetation. Curtains of *Hedera* (ivy) or clematis can look very dramatic. One effective use is to train them along and over a balustrade or fence. However, if the balustrade is a handrail placed there for safety purposes it is best to leave it clear, especially if there are elderly people around who may depend on it. *Clematis montana* will form a thick curtain of purplish vegetation with flowers in spring.

MAKING A "FEDGE"

A fedge is a mixture of a fence and a hedge. It consists of a wire-netting fence over which ivy is allowed to grow. When the ivy covers the whole structure, it is clipped just like a hedge. It is a good way to cover an ugly fence or make a quick hedge. The ivy could all be the same variety, but a more interesting pattern can be achieved by using a gold-leaved or variegated form every three plants or so.

PROJECT   **CLIMBER CURTAINS**

1 Dig three holes at least 18in (45cm) deep, at 4ft (1.2m) intervals. Place an upright post in each and backfill the gaps with rammed earth or use concrete for extra security.

2 Use galvanized nails to attach a rail across the tops of the posts. Plant a *Clematis montana* against the center post and use string or plastic-covered wire to hold the stems in place.

3 When the clematis shoots reach the top of the post, train them along the rail on either side. Again, use string or plastic-covered wire.

4 It will soon become self-supporting and travel along the rails in either direction, as well as hanging down in a thick curtain of foliage.

PROJECT   **CREATING A FEDGE**

 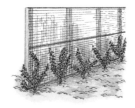 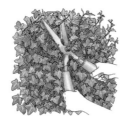

1 Erect a fence with upright posts, as above, and a heavy wire along the top, middle, and bottom. Use these wires to support the wire mesh.

2 Position ivy plants at 36in (90cm) intervals along the fence. Dig the planting holes and mix in some organic material, then plant the ivies.

3 When the ivies have completely covered the netting, shear them over once or twice a year to keep them looking neat and tidy.

STAR PLANTS

- *Clematis montana*
- *Fallopia bald-schuanica* (Russian vine)
- *Hedera helix* (ivy)
- *Humulus lupulus* 'Aureus' (golden hop)
- *Parthenocissus henryana* (Chinese virginia creeper)
- *Vitis vinifera* 'Purpurea' (purple-leaved grape)

THE PLANT DIRECTORY

Foliage is a vital component in any garden. It may create a rich dark evergreen background to set off the brighter colors of spring and summer flowers, or become the visual attraction in its own right in its strikingly colored or variegated forms, especially in autumn. Some leaves are distinctive in other ways as well, such as their size and shape, from the huge leaves of *Gunnera manicata* (giant rhubarb) to the graceful arching fronds of ferns. Some foliage plants are also invaluable for use as ground cover.

LEFT *Beautiful effects can be easily achieved just by combining foliage plants that exhibit complementary colors such as green and gold.*

HOW TO USE THIS DIRECTORY

The Plant Directory lists all the plants that are featured in this book, together with a selection of other plants that are suitable for use in a foliage garden. It is not intended to be exhaustive, and experienced gardeners will have their own favorites. However, this listing has been made with the specific requirements of a foliage garden in mind, and will guide the beginner to a range of attractive and readily available plants, shrubs, and trees with which to create a beautiful garden. Complete information on planting and maintaining the plants is given for each entry.

The Plant Directory is divided into several different categories that group similar plants together. The various categories are as follows: annuals and biennials *(pages 62–65),* bulbs *(pages 66–67),* herbaceous perennials *(pages 68–83),* grasses *(pages 84–87),* bamboos *(pages 88–89),* ferns *(pages 90–93),* trees and shrubs *(pages 94–105)* and finally climbers *(pages 106–107).*

Each entry is illustrated with a color photograph to help you choose the right foliage plant for any given situation. The symbols panel accompanying each entry gives essential information on growing conditions and requirements. Unless otherwise stated in the plant description, the plant will tolerate any type of soil, but will probably do best when grown in a fertile, well-drained one.

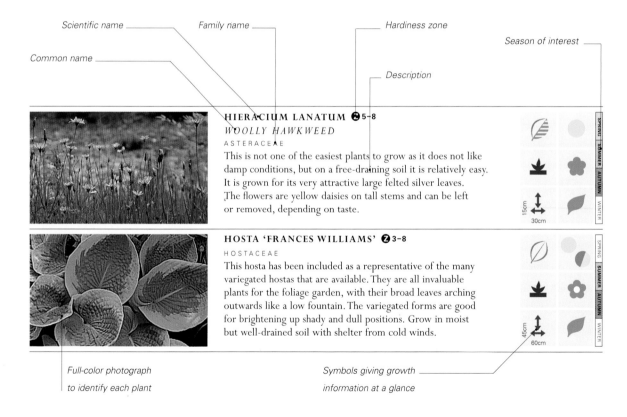

Scientific name

Common name

Family name

Hardiness zone

Description

Season of interest

HIERACIUM LANATUM ❷ 5–8
WOOLLY HAWKWEED
ASTERACEAE
This is not one of the easiest plants to grow as it does not like damp conditions, but on a free-draining soil it is relatively easy. It is grown for its very attractive large felted silver leaves. The flowers are yellow daisies on tall stems and can be left or removed, depending on taste.

SPRING SUMMER AUTUMN WINTER
15cm 30cm

HOSTA 'FRANCES WILLIAMS' ❷ 3–8
HOSTACEAE
This hosta has been included as a representative of the many variegated hostas that are available. They are all invaluable plants for the foliage garden, with their broad leaves arching outwards like a low fountain. The variegated forms are good for brightening up shady and dull positions. Grow in moist but well-drained soil with shelter from cold winds.

SPRING SUMMER AUTUMN WINTER
45cm 60cm

Full-color photograph to identify each plant

Symbols giving growth information at a glance

KEY TO THE SYMBOLS

 EASY TO GROW

These are tolerant plants that require no special care or conditions in order to flourish.

 MODERATE TO GROW

These are plants that require some special care, such as protection from frost.

 DIFFICULT TO GROW

These are plants that require a great deal of specialized care, and offer a challenge for the more experienced gardener.

 EVERGREEN

 SEMI-EVERGREEN

 DECIDUOUS

Deciduous plants lose all their leaves in autumn (sometimes in summer) while evergreen plants keep their foliage all the year round. Plants described as semi-evergreen may keep some or all of their foliage through the winter in sheltered gardens or if the weather is mild. No leaf symbol is given for annuals, nor for biennials, although some biennials do keep their leaves over the first winter.

 FEATURE LEAVES

 FEATURE SCENT

 FEATURE FLOWER

 FEATURE FRUIT

These symbols indicate the main feature of interest for each plant in the directory. This will help you to choose plants that have complementary features, or plants that will perform a specific function in your garden. The symbols show the main feature of interest, but this is not necessarily the plant's only attractive asset.

 RAPID GROWTH

 MODERATE GROWTH

 SLOW GROWTH

Speed of growth, like ease of growth, is a highly subjective category, and will vary according to local conditions. Rapid growth indicates plants that reach their full extent in a single season (annuals for instance), or plants that make substantial progress towards filling the space allowed for them in a single season. Slow growth indicates plants, such as trees and some shrubs, that take several seasons to reach their ultimate size. Moderate growth refers therefore to rates of progress between these two extremes.

The period of the year when a plant is likely to be at its most attractive is also indicated. This will allow you, for instance, to create a planting scheme that will have something of interest for each season of the year.

 HEIGHT AND SPREAD

The size of plants will vary according to the growing conditions in your garden, so these measurements are a rough guide only. In all cases the measurements refer to the size of plants and trees when mature, although again there are specific cases where the ultimate size is never reached. For instance, bedding and climbing roses can be pruned to fit smaller spaces, and the spread of water plants may be governed largely by the size of the pond they are planted in. When the spread of the plant is indefinite it is marked 6ft.

 FULL SUN

 PARTIAL SUN

 SHADE

An indication of light preference is given to show each plant's optimum growing situation. Here again, this is only a rough guide, as some plants that prefer sun may also be reasonably tolerant of shade.

ANNUALS AND BIENNIALS

ALTERNANTHERA FICOIDEA **Z** 2-11
JOSEPH'S COAT
AMARANTHACEAE

This genus contains several species and cultivars which are used in foliage bedding schemes. They are ideal for creating a flat area of one color. The various cultivars of *A. ficoidea* in particular are available in many colors including light green, red, copper, and yellow. Keep clipped.

ARGEMONE MEXICANA **Z** 2-11
PRICKLY POPPY
PAPAVERACEAE

The prickly poppy is grown mainly for its yellow tissue-paper-like flowers, but it also has very attractive foliage which is blue-green with silver veins running through it. The thistle-like leaves are deeply cut and have prickly spines on the tips. The seed pods are also attractive but similarly barbed.

ATRIPLEX HORTENSIS VAR. RUBRA **Z** 2-11
RED MOUNTAIN SPINACH
CHENOPODIACEAE

A quick-growing, tall annual with a reddish purple foliage. When young the leaves can be eaten. It makes an excellent plant to dot around in a border when touches of purple are needed to calm down a color scheme. It self-sows, providing a ready supply of seedlings each year.

BASSIA SCOPARIA F. TRICHOPHYLLA **Z** 2-11
BURNING BUSH
CHENOPODIACEAE

Also known as *Kochia tricophylla*, burning bushes are wonderful foliage plants, although not so popular as they once were. They form a rounded or cone-shaped "bush" with fresh green leaves and inconspicuous flowers. In autumn, the foliage turns red. They make good bedding plants, but can be used in mixed borders.

BETA VULGARIS 'RUBY CHARD' **Z** 3-11
CHENOPODIACEAE

This plant is really a vegetable—one of the Swiss chards—but this particular variety is also frequently grown in the ornamental garden because of its decorative foliage. The leaves are a deep purple-bronze and the leaf stalks are a brilliant red. It is best grown in a place where the evening light strikes it. You can also cook and eat the leaves.

BORAGO OFFICINALIS **Z** 3-9
BORAGE
BORAGINACEAE

Borage is mainly grown for its delightful blue flowers, which are often used as decoration in cooking. The foliage also has a part to play, however, especially in wilder parts of the garden. It is a somewhat floppy plant with large grayish leaves, covered in coarse bristles, that are good for filling gaps.

| 〰 leaf type | light preference | ⚓ speed of growth | ⚙ ease of growth |

BRASSICA OLERACEA Ⓩ 1–11
ORNAMENTAL KALE
BRASSICACEAE

Although it can be eaten, this kale is mainly grown for winter decoration. It forms a tight cabbage with layers of leaves gently opening like a giant rose. The leaves vary in color from purple through to cream. It is valuable for creating foliage effects in containers and borders during the winter months.

12in / 12in

ERYNGIUM GIGANTEUM Ⓩ 5–8
MISS WILLMOTT'S GHOST
APIACEAE

This is a short-lived perennial that is usually treated as a biennial. It has stiff leathery leaves that are deeply divided and have prickly tips. The leaves are mid-green with silver veins, turning paler as the summer progresses, until they are almost white. The flowers appear in clusters of steely blue. It likes a well-drained situation.

18in / 12in

EUPHORBIA LATHYRIS Ⓩ 6–9
CAPER SPURGE
EUPHORBIACEAE

This is a valuable architectural plant, creating a tree-like effect quite unlike any other plant. The gray-green leaves are tapered, giving the plant a stiff look. It can be used in isolation or added to a border for dramatic effect. Although called caper spurge because its seed pods look like capers, they are in fact poisonous.

5ft / 30in

EUPHORBIA MARGINATA Ⓩ 2–11
SNOW ON THE MOUNTAIN
EUPHORBIACEAE

A delightful annual grown for its icy-white variegated foliage. When young, the leaves are green, but gradually acquire white margins which get broader towards the top of the plant. It produces a number of upright stems from a single crown. The flowers are relatively insignificant.

20in / 12in

GALACTITES TOMENTOSA` Ⓩ 2–11
MEDITERRANEAN THISTLE
ASTERACEAE

A superb annual with prickly thistle-like leaves that are covered in a delicate tracery of silver markings. The plant has soft purple thistle flowers. It is a very airy-looking plant, and looks best in a border mixed in with other plants. It self-sows moderately, so there are often enough seedlings for future years.

3ft / 2ft

HELICHRYSUM PETIOLARE Ⓩ 10–11
LIQUORICE PLANT
ASTERACEAE

Although always treated as an annual, this is a perennial bush. It is grown for its matte gray foliage which appears on stems that ramble among and through other plants. It is mainly grown as a foil. The flowers are insignificant. There are several cultivars of which 'Limelight' has lime-green foliage.

2ft / 2ft

↕ height and spread   ✳ feature of interest   ▭ season of interest   *ANNUALS A—H*

ANNUALS AND BIENNIALS

LOTUS BERTHELOTTI ❷ 9–10
PARROT'S BEAK
PAPILIONACEAE

A shrubby perennial that is treated as an annual. It is grown for its superb silver filigree foliage. It can be grown on the ground but looks best when tumbling from a container or hanging basket. It also produces red flowers, but these are over by early summer. Take cuttings in summer for next year's plants.

LUNARIA ANNUA 'ALBA VARIEGATA' ❷ 5–9
VARIEGATED HONESTY
BRASSICACEAE

The leaves of the species itself are not particularly interesting, but the foliage of the variegated forms makes them well worth growing. This cultivar is the most striking of all, especially when the plant is covered in white flowers in late spring. It is excellent for brightening a dark corner.

MOLUCCELLA LAEVIS ❷ 2–11
BELLS OF IRELAND
LAMIACEAE

This is a useful plant for cooling down bedding schemes. The white flowers are insignificant, hidden by leafy bracts. The scalloped leaves and the bracts are a pale green, and they turn pale brown as the plant comes into fruit. The cut flowers are good when dried.

ONOPORDUM ACANTHIUM ❷ 6–9
SCOTCH THISTLE
ASTERACEAE

A very dramatic plant with wide prickly wings to the stems and prickly thistle-like leaves. All the foliage and stems are bright silver. It produces purple flowers, but is mainly grown for the foliage. Several other species, for example *O. nervosum,* are similar in effect. It self-sows.

RICINUS COMMUNIS CULTIVARS ❷ 9–10
CASTOR OIL PLANT
EUPHORBIACEAE

This is a perennial shrub, but it is usually treated as an annual, grown from seed. It has large palmate leaves which vary in colour according to the cultivar. Some are green, others bronze, and some purple or red. It is mainly used as an accent plant. Handle with gloves as it can provoke a serious allergic reaction.

SALVIA ARGENTEA ❷ 5–8
SILVER SALVIA
LAMIACEAE

This is a spectacular foliage plant, especially in its first year, when it forms a large rosette. The large leaves are covered with woolly hairs and are very silver. Unfortunately they are delicate and can be easily damaged by the weather. They need a hot, well-drained position to perform well.

🌿 leaf type   ● light preference   ⚓ speed of growth   ⚙ ease of growth

SENECIO CINERARIA 8–10
ASTERACEAE

This is a perennial shrub that is normally treated as an annual in gardens. It is grown for its deeply lobed silver foliage. It produces yellow flowers, but these are usually removed as they can look untidy. It is a good plant for use in bedding schemes, creating a foil against which to display the other colors. It is also known as *S. maritimus*.

12in
12in

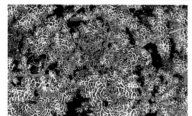

SILYBUM MARIANUM 6–9
MILK THISTLE
ASTERACEAE

A very distinct thistle with large cabbagy leaves that are bright green with very pronounced white or silver patterns on them. It will eventually flower, but it is the foliage that it is grown for. It works best in a mixed border although in a rich soil it can be grown as a specimen plant.

3ft
3ft

SOLENOSTEMON SCUTELLARIOIDES 2–11
COLEUS
LAMIACEAE

Also known as *Coleus blumei*, this is a well-known house plant that makes a good summer bedding plant. The leaves come in a wide variety of greens, yellows, browns, oranges, and reds. They can be used in a border or set out in containers. Cuttings can be taken and overwintered to provide new plants.

2ft
2ft

TROPAEOLUM MAJUS 'ALASKA' 2–11
NASTURTIUM
TROPAEOLACEAE

Most nasturtiums can be grown for their round foliage which contrasts well when grown through other plants. This cultivar has leaves that are splashed with yellow making them show up, especially in shady areas. It has the usual red, orange, or yellow nasturtium flowers as a bonus.

3ft
3ft

VERBASCUM BOMBYCIFERUM 4–8
MULLEIN
SCROPHULARIACEAE

This is a biennial that is particularly valuable as a foliage plant during its first year as it has very large silver leaves. In its second year, the foliage is still very good, but the towering yellow flower spike tends to grab the attention. It is a good plant for giving height to a mixed border.

8ft
30in

VERBASCUM OLYMPICUM 5–9
MULLEIN
SCROPHULARACEAE

This mullein is a very imposing plant with silver foliage and stems, and a towering spire of yellow flowers. It often has side stems, much in the manner of a large candelabra. It is a short-lived perennial, but it usually dies after flowering in its second year, so it is treated as a biennial.

6ft
2ft

---

 height and spread   feature of interest    season of interest   *ANNUALS L–V*

BULBS

ARUM ITALICUM 'MARMORATUM' Z 6-9
ITALIAN LORDS AND LADIES
ARACEAE

A very distinct plant for growing in shady places. The typical broad pointed arum leaves have a silver marking delicately traced over them. The leaves appear in early winter and are not troubled by frost, making them valuable for foliage decoration at that time of year. A good woodland plant.

CARDIOCRINUM GIGANTEUM Z 7-9
GIANT LILY
LILIACEAE

The giant lily is grown mainly for its white trumpet flowers, but these can take up to seven years or more to appear and in the mean time it makes a useful foliage plant. It is a tall plant with large triangular leaves. It is good for growing among shrubs to create a vertical emphasis.

CORYDALIS SOLIDA Z 5-7
FUMEWORT
PAPAVERACEAE

A small plant with very delicate, almost filigree leaves, much in the manner of a dicentra. They only appear above ground during the spring, but at a time when there is little other foliage around. This is basically a woodland plant and therefore good for growing in shady areas.

CROCOSMIA MASONIORUM Z 7-9
MONTBRETIA
IRIDACEAE

A tall form of montbretia with long strap-like leaves. In this species the leaves are wide and have distinctive raised veins on them. The long slightly arching stems make a good contrast with other more solid plants. It has bright orange-red flowers in late summer. Autumn color is also good.

CYCLAMEN COUM Z 5-9
EASTERN CYCLAMEN
PRIMULACEAE

This is a very valuable cyclamen whose leaves appear in early winter and continue until the spring. They are almost circular and often have dainty silver markings on them. They are not individually very large but make a good spread en masse. The magenta flowers appear in midwinter.

CYCLAMEN HEDERIFOLIUM Z 8-9
PRIMULACEAE

This is the commonest of the hardy cyclamens. Although it is often grown for its pink late-summer or early-autumn flowers, it makes a very impressive foliage plant from that time of year right round to the start of the following summer. The leaves are ivy-shaped, often with silver markings. They can form extensive carpets, making them useful for ground cover.

≣ leaf type   ○ light preference   ♨ speed of growth   ✿ ease of growth

DAHLIA 'BISHOP OF LLANDAFF' **Z** 8–10
ASTERACEAE

Dahlias are not generally grown for their foliage, but this cultivar has superb bronze/purple leaves and is frequently used in mixed borders where this foliage color is required. It is also sometimes used as a bedding plant. The flowers are a dark red, which complements the foliage perfectly. It is best stored under cover during the winter.

ERYTHRONIUM DENS-CANIS **Z** 3–9
DOG-TOOTH VIOLET
LILIACEAE

Several of the erythroniums have attractive foliage but this is one of the best. The soft grayish-green leaves are mottled with purple. They only appear during the spring, but make good ground cover for a lightly shaded place during their short season. The nodding flowers are pinkish-purple.

LILIUM PYRENAICUM **Z** 4–7
PYRENEAN LILY
LILIACEAE

Many of the lilies have attractive foliage, but in this species it becomes quite distinctive with masses of whorls of narrow leaves up the whole stem. The leaves are a fresh light green. The flowers are of the turks-cap type, and they are yellow, which goes well with the foliage in early summer.

RANUNCULUS FICARIA 'BRAZEN HUSSY' **Z** 4–8
LESSER CELANDINE
RANUNCULACEAE

Several of the celandines have interesting foliage but this is the most distinctive. The leaves are a dark rich bronze. This contrasts beautifully with the bright yellow flowers, especially when the sun shines. The foliage appears in early to midwinter and continues well into spring. It spreads.

TRILLIUM SESSILE **Z** 4–8
WOOD LILY
TRILLIACEAE

A superb plant for growing in drifts in light woodland. The three leaves are in a whorl just below the three petals. The leaves are mid-green and mottled with dark green, almost black. They appear in late winter and continue through spring. The flowers are three erect petals, usually of bright red.

TROPAEOLUM POLYPHYLLUM **Z** 8–10
ROCK NASTURTIUM
TROPAEOLACEAE

An unusual but superb nasturtium with long trailing stems of silver leaves. The stems have a habit of spreading underground and coming up some way from the original bulb. It is best planted under a rock to give it some winter protection. The flowers are the typical nasturtium shape, but smaller and orange.

 height and spread ✳ feature of interest  season of interest *BULBS A—T*

HERBACEOUS PERENNIALS

ACAENA MICROPHYLLA ⓩ 6–6
NEW ZEALAND BUR
ROSACEAE
The acaenas are attractive low ground-covering plants. Several have attractive foliage as well as the globular flowers and bur-like seed heads. This species has gray-green leaves that are tinted bronze. One of the best acaenas is *A. saccaticupula* 'Blue Haze' which has slatey-blue foliage that forms large carpets.

ACANTHUS MOLLIS ⓩ 7–10
BEAR'S BREECHES
ACANTHACEAE
This has deeply cut leaves, but lacks the spines that adorn *A. spinosus*. The broad, dully shining expanse of the leaves makes it an interesting foliage plant, contrasting well with those plants with leaves that have a more regular outline. The attractive tall flower spikes of purple hooded blooms last a long time.

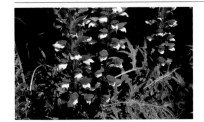

ACANTHUS SPINOSUS ⓩ 5–9
BEAR'S BREECHES
ACANTHACEAE
This is a dramatic plant that can be used as an accent plant in a border or as a specimen, possibly in a large container. The leaves are jagged, ending in prickles, somewhat like a thistle. The hooded flowers are carried on tall spikes. The form 'Spinosissimus' has more prickly and deeply cut leaves.

ACIPHYLLA AUREA ⓩ 8–10
GOLDEN SPANIARD
APIACEAE
This plant is distinguished by its fountain of very stiff narrow leaves. The end of each leaf ends in a vicious point which makes weeding near them very uncomfortable; because of this some gardeners avoid them. However, they do make a wonderful spray of foliage and can be used in a mixed border or in a container.

ACONITUM CARMICHAELII ⓩ 3–7
MONKSHOOD
RANUNCULACEAE
The monkshoods are grown for their hooded blue or yellow flowers. There are some autumn-flowering species like this, however, that provide a good display of foliage before they flower. They create a large clump of deeply divided leaves, rather like delphiniums. This is a poisonous plant.

ACORUS CALAMUS 'VARIEGATUS' ⓩ 4–11
SWEET FLAG
ARACEAE
This is a plant that is suitable for growing in shallow water in a bog garden. The foliage is strap-like, similar to that of an iris. The species is green, but in this variety the leaves are striped in cream right along their length, and are often flushed pink in spring. The foliage is also scented.

🌿 leaf type   ◯ light preference   🌱 speed of growth   ✿ ease of growth

AGAVE AMERICANA 'VARIEGATA' ● 2–11
CENTURY PLANT
AGAVACEAE

This is a rather coarse plant, but plays a vital part in dry gardens. It forms a basal rosette from which arise succulent blue-green leaves with the edges marked in yellow. The leaves are sharply pointed and have spines on the margins. It is marginally tender and is best grown in containers that can be moved inside.

AJUGA REPTANS ❷ 3–9
BUGLE
LAMIACEAE

A very good ground-covering plant for light shade. The species has green leaves and spikes of blue flowers in spring, but there are several cultivars with more attractive foliage. 'Atropurpurea' has dark purple leaves, and 'Multicolor' has variegated leaves in pink and cream. Bugle does best in a moist soil.

ALCHEMILLA MOLLIS ❷ 4–7
LADY'S MANTLE
ROSACEAE

One of the most versatile foliage plants with soft pleated leaves overtopped by plumes of yellowish-green flowers. It makes excellent ground cover and looks particularly good flopping over a path or wall, or beside a water feature. It should be cut to the ground after flowering to promote fresh foliage.

ANAPHALIS MARGARITACEA ❷ 4–8
PEARLY EVERLASTING
ASTERACEAE

Although sometimes grown for its everlasting flowers, the main interest in anaphalis in the border is its grayish-green foliage. It is useful for creating blocks of silver color for uniting different colors. Its close relative *A. triplinervis* has more silvery foliage. Neither will grow in the shade.

ARTEMISIA ABSINTHIUM 'LAMBROOK SILVER' ❷ 4–8
ASTERACEAE

This is a beautiful foliage plant with deeply divided leaves which are very silvery in color. They are also aromatic. It is an extremely good plant for the herbaceous or mixed border and mixes with a variety of colors. The flowers, produced in late summer, are muddy-colored and are usually removed as they detract from the appearance of the plant.

ARTEMISIA ALBA 'CANESCENS' ❷ 4–8
ASTERACEAE

This is a plant with very finely cut foliage. Like most other artemisias the foliage is silver, but the great attraction of this plant is the curly filigree nature of the leaves. It makes a dense low bush and is a perfect foil in a mixed or herbaceous border. The brownish-yellow flowers that appear in late summer are insignificant and may be removed.

---

‡ height and spread   ✳ feature of interest   ▮▮▮▮ season of interest   *HERBACEOUS PERENNIALS* **A**

HERBACEOUS PERENNIALS

ARTEMISIA LUDOVICIANA ❷4–9
ASTERACEAE

This artemisia is different from the others in that it has more solid, willow-like leaves. It is also taller. However, the color is still silvery and it often looks like pewter. The flower stems, which appear from midsumer to autumn, detract from the plant and are usually removed. Two of the best forms of this plant are 'Silver Queen' and 'Valerie Finnis'.

ARTEMISIA 'POWIS CASTLE' ❷7–9
ASTERACEAE

This is one of the great plants of the herbaceous garden. The foliage is very delicately cut. It has a very soft feel to it and is bright shining silver, one of the most silver of all plants. It produces a mass of foliage and only a few insignificant flowers in late summer. It is not long-lasting and will need to be replaced every few years.

ARUNCUS DIOICUS ❷3–7
GOATSBEARD
ROSACEAE

When in bloom, the creamy flowers are the focus of attention, but goatsbeard also makes an excellent foliage plant. The leaves are divided into individual leaflets, each novel in shape and pleated. In the form 'Kneiffii' they are deeply cut, creating a delicately filmy foliage. They like a moist soil.

ASARUM EUROPAEUM ❷4–8
ASARABACCA
ARISTOLOCHIACEAE

This plant can be overlooked in a garden simply because it is so good at doing its job. It is a low-growing plant with kidney-shaped leaves that are very glossy and mid- to dark green. They make perfect carpets of ground cover in a shady area. It has hidden flowers in spring.

ASTILBE X ARENDSII ❷4–8
SAXIFRAGACEAE

Astilbes are generally grown for their frothy flower heads, but they also make very good foliage plants, especially in bog gardens or beside ponds. The leaves are compound, made up of individual leaflets, which give a nice texture when grown as a large group. There are many varieties, in flower colors ranging from white or cream through pink to crimson.

ASTILBOIDES TABULARIS ❷5–7
SAXIFRAGACEAE

A close relative of the rodgersias, this is a good plant for the middle of a border where a contrast of leaf shape is required. It produces large round leaves that can be 36in (90cm) across, which are supported by a central stem, like a parasol. It has creamy flowers held well above the leaves. It grows best in cool, moist soil in partial shade.

⫴ leaf type   ● light preference   ⚱ speed of growth   ✿ ease of growth

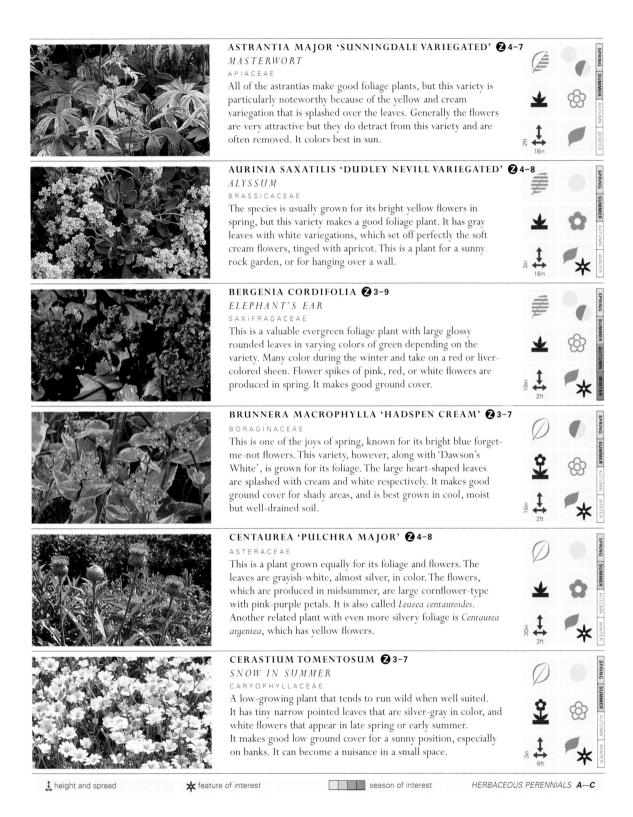

ASTRANTIA MAJOR 'SUNNINGDALE VARIEGATED' Ⓩ 4–7
MASTERWORT
APIACEAE

All of the astrantias make good foliage plants, but this variety is particularly noteworthy because of the yellow and cream variegation that is splashed over the leaves. Generally the flowers are very attractive but they do detract from this variety and are often removed. It colors best in sun.

2ft · 18in

AURINIA SAXATILIS 'DUDLEY NEVILL VARIEGATED' Ⓩ 4–8
ALYSSUM
BRASSICACEAE

The species is usually grown for its bright yellow flowers in spring, but this variety makes a good foliage plant. It has gray leaves with white variegations, which set off perfectly the soft cream flowers, tinged with apricot. This is a plant for a sunny rock garden, or for hanging over a wall.

3in · 18in

BERGENIA CORDIFOLIA Ⓩ 3–9
ELEPHANT'S EAR
SAXIFRAGACEAE

This is a valuable evergreen foliage plant with large glossy rounded leaves in varying colors of green depending on the variety. Many color during the winter and take on a red or liver-colored sheen. Flower spikes of pink, red, or white flowers are produced in spring. It makes good ground cover.

18in · 2ft

BRUNNERA MACROPHYLLA 'HADSPEN CREAM' Ⓩ 3–7
BORAGINACEAE

This is one of the joys of spring, known for its bright blue forget-me-not flowers. This variety, however, along with 'Dawson's White', is grown for its foliage. The large heart-shaped leaves are splashed with cream and white respectively. It makes good ground cover for shady areas, and is best grown in cool, moist but well-drained soil.

18in · 2ft

CENTAUREA 'PULCHRA MAJOR' Ⓩ 4–8
ASTERACEAE

This is a plant grown equally for its foliage and flowers. The leaves are grayish-white, almost silver, in color. The flowers, which are produced in midsummer, are large cornflower-type with pink-purple petals. It is also called *Leuzea centauroides*. Another related plant with even more silvery foliage is *Centaurea argentea*, which has yellow flowers.

30in · 2ft

CERASTIUM TOMENTOSUM Ⓩ 3–7
SNOW IN SUMMER
CARYOPHYLLACEAE

A low-growing plant that tends to run wild when well suited. It has tiny narrow pointed leaves that are silver-gray in color, and white flowers that appear in late spring or early summer. It makes good low ground cover for a sunny position, especially on banks. It can become a nuisance in a small space.

3in · 6ft

SPRING · SUMMER · AUTUMN · WINTER

↕ height and spread ✳ feature of interest ▮▮▮ season of interest *HERBACEOUS PERENNIALS* **A—C**

HERBACEOUS PERENNIALS

CHAMAEMELUM NOBILE 'TRENEAGUE' ❷ 6–9
ROMAN CHAMOMILE
ASTERACEAE

This variety of chamomile is very useful as it lacks the usual white daisy-like flowers and is used purely as a foliage plant. It is also low-growing and hardwearing and so can be used for chamomile lawns and chamomile seats, as well as other situations where a carpet of green is required. It is fragrant when crushed.

CLEMATIS RECTA 'PURPUREA' ❷ 3–7
RANUNCULACEAE

This is a herbaceous clematis that dies back to the ground each year. The species has green leaves, but this variety is grown for its dark purple foliage. It forms a mound that needs staking. The flowers are very small and creamy-colored, and are produced from midsummer to autumn. It is a good plant for placing in the middle of a mixed border.

CONVALLARIA MAJALIS 'VARIEGATA' ❷ 2–7
LILY OF THE VALLEY
CONVALLARIACEAE

The lily of the valley is an old garden favorite. The green leaves form good ground cover but are not especially attractive. However, this variety has yellow-striped leaves that have a wonderful fresh-looking quality about them. They have the usual attractive fragrant bell-shaped flowers.

CRAMBE MARITIMA ❷ 6–9
SEA CABBAGE
BRASSICACEAE

A low mound-forming plant with wonderful glaucous blue-green foliage. The leaves are thick and fleshy and have an interesting twist in them. It has sprays of honey-scented white flowers in spring. It is good for dry and Mediterranean gardens. Its relative *C. cordifolia* is a much bigger plant with large green leaves.

CYNARA CARDUNCULUS ❷ 7–9
CARDOON
ASTERACEAE

A splendid foliage plant with huge deeply cut bright silver leaves that arch out from the bottom of the plant. It is tall and capped with large purple thistle-like flowers. Its architectural qualities make it one of the most important, as either an accent or a specimen plant.

DARMERA PELTATA ❷ 5–9
UMBRELLA PLANT
SAXIFRAGACEAE

Also known as *Peltiphyllum peltatum*, this is the perfect plant for ground cover in a large garden, but should be avoided in smaller ones. It has large round leaves that are 12in (30cm) or more across. The pink flowers appear first on tall naked stems, followed by the leaves. It needs a damp soil.

 leaf type   light preference   🌱 speed of growth   ⚘ ease of growth

DELPHINIUM ELATUM GROUP ⓩ 3–10

RANUNCULACEAE

There are hundreds of different delphinium hybrids which, although they vary slightly in flower color, all have the same type of foliage. It is the flowers that are the main attraction, but before and after flowering the clumps of green lobed leaves make an attractive border feature. Delphiniums will grow in any fertile, well-drained soil.

SPRING SUMMER AUTUMN WINTER

6ft / 3ft

DIANTHUS 'MRS SINKINS' ⓩ 2–9

PINK

CARYOPHYLLACEAE

Pinks are grown mainly for their flowers, but many of the old-fashioned varieties, such as 'Mrs Sinkins', only have a short season and for the rest of the time they form a very good mat of silver foliage known as "grass." Remove the old flower stems. They like a well-drained soil that is neutral or alkaline.

SPRING SUMMER AUTUMN WINTER

6in / 2ft

ERYNGIUM AGAVIFOLIUM ⓩ 6–9

APIACEAE

The foliage of this plant is very distinctive. It forms a rosette from which long sword-like leaves curve outwards. They are stiff and edged with vicious barbs. They make a good contrast to smoother leaves, but care must be taken when weeding near them. The whitish flowers appear in late summer on tall stems. It prefers a moist but well-drained soil.

SPRING SUMMER AUTUMN WINTER

5ft / 2ft

ERYNGIUM VARIIFOLIUM ⓩ 5–9

VARIEGATED SEA HOLLY

APIACEAE

The sea hollies make excellent foliage plants because most have attractive thistle-like leaves and bracts. Some have arching strap-like leaves, usually heavily barbed. This species and the related *E. bourgatii* have the advantage in that they have attractive silver markings on the leaves.

SPRING SUMMER AUTUMN WINTER

18in / 10in

EUPHORBIA CHARACIAS ⓩ 7–10

MEDITERRANEAN SPURGE

EUPHORBIACEAE

This is a large spurge that forms a big clump, although it is not invasive. It has narrow leaves extending horizontally all up the tall stems. It mixes in well in a border or makes a fine specimen plant. It looks particularly good on corners. The subspecies *E. c.* subsp. *wulfenii* is even more attractive.

SPRING SUMMER AUTUMN WINTER

4ft / 3ft

EUPHORBIA GRIFFITHII ⓩ 4–9

EUPHORBIACEAE

This is an upright euphorbia with red midribs and stems to the foliage, which also takes on autumn tints. The bracts round the insignificant flowers are also red. This plant is usually seen in one of its two cultivars 'Fireglow' or 'Dixter', both of which are more colored than the species. It can spread vigorously in lighter soils.

SPRING SUMMER AUTUMN WINTER

3ft / 2ft

---

 height and spread   ✳ feature of interest    season of interest   *HERBACEOUS PERENNIALS* **C—E**

HERBACEOUS PERENNIALS

EUPHORBIA MYRSINITES ⓩ 5–8
EUPHORBIACEAE

This is a low-growing euphorbia with spreading stems covered in spirals of blue-green leaves. The leaves are pointed and fleshy. It has flower heads in spring that are colored by the yellow bracts rather than the insignificant flowers. It is a particularly good foliage plant for the rock garden, because it does not grow very tall, swamping the other plants.

8in 18in

EUPHORBIA POLYCHROMA ⓩ 4–9
EUPHORBIACEAE

A euphorbia that is at its best in spring when it forms a perfect rounded dome of foliage topped by bright yellow bracts. Later the bracts fade and the leaves loses their freshness, but it still makes a good foliage plant through until autumn. It can be used as a border plant. 'Candy' has purple foliage, but is not such a strong plant.

18in 2ft

FERULA COMMUNIS ⓩ 6–9
GIANT FENNEL
APIACEAE

As its name suggests, giant fennel is a relative of fennel (*Foeniculum vulgare*). The bright green leaves are large and very finely cut so that they are feathery in appearance. It acts as an attractive foliage plant for several years and then produces tall flower spikes. Sometimes the plant dies after flowering.

10ft 3ft

FILIPENDULA ULMARIA 'AUREA' ⓩ 3–9
GOLDEN MEADOWSWEET
ROSACEAE

Most filipendulas are grown for the froth of sweet-smelling flowers that they produce in late summer. However, this form is grown for its foliage which is yellow-green in the spring, becoming creamier as the summer progresses. The flowers are usually removed. It prefers a moist soil.

3ft 12in

FOENICULUM VULGARE 'PURPUREUM' ⓩ 4–9
BRONZE FENNEL
APIACEAE

This is an important foliage plant. It has very finely cut filigree leaves that are a beautiful bronze color. This soft foliage is carried on tall slender stems. The whole plant makes an impact and can be used in a variety of ways in the border. It has small yellow flowers which tend to seed everywhere.

6ft 2ft

FRAGARIA X ANANASSA 'VARIEGATA' ⓩ 3–9
VARIEGATED STRAWBERRY
ROSACEAE

Strawberries are not usually thought of as decorative plants, but this variety is. It has conventional strawberry leaves, except that they are heavily splashed with bright cream markings. The plant spreads by runner to make effective ground cover, especially among shrubs where its cream markings shine out.

4in 2ft

≡ leaf type	● light preference	⚡ speed of growth	✿ ease of growth

GALAX URCEOLATA ⓩ 5–8
WANDFLOWER
DIAPENSIACEAE

This is a good dense ground-cover plant for shady areas. It forms a carpet of round glossy leaves that turn dark red in autumn. During early summer, airy spikes of white flowers appear, held well above the foliage. Being a woodland plant it likes an acid, humus-rich soil that never completely dries out.

12in / 3ft

GERANIUM MACRORRHIZUM ⓩ 4–8
GERANIACEAE

This is one of the best plants for growing as ground cover beneath the canopy of trees. It makes a dense carpet of slightly furry leaves that have a distinctive smell when they are crushed. It will grow in most conditions, including dry ones, and will also tolerate a surprising amount of shade. It has purple, pink, or white flowers in spring.

12in / 2ft

GERANIUM PHAEUM 'SAMOBOR' ⓩ 4–8
DUSKY CRANESBILL
GERANIACEAE

Although the flowers are attractive, this cultivar is grown mainly for its foliage. The soft green lobed leaves in the species are not particularly distinguished, but in this form they have a large deep bronze marking. These make it an interesting foliage plant even when it is not in flower.

18in / 18in

GERANIUM RENARDII ⓩ 6–8
GERANIACEAE

This geranium is usually grown for its foliage rather than its flowers, although the latter are relatively attractive. The leaves are roundish in shape, with shallow lobes and a wrinkled surface. The main attraction is that they are gray. It is a low-growing plant, and comes in very useful in instances where gray foliage is required at the front of a border.

9in / 18in

GUNNERA MANICATA ⓩ 7–10
GIANT RHUBARB
GUNNERACEAE

This is one of the largest herbaceous garden plants. It has enormous leaves, up to 6ft (1.8m) or more across, often held above head height, making it possible to shelter underneath. It likes a moist situation and is often planted next to a pond, frequently as a specimen plant.

7ft / 10ft

HEMEROCALLIS SPECIES AND HYBRIDS ⓩ 3–10
DAY LILIES
HEMEROCALLIDACEAE

There are a great many different species and hybrids of day lily, which, although they have different flowers, all have roughly the same type of foliage. The leaves are strap-like, cascading out like a loose fountain. They make a contrast to other plants in either a mixed or herbaceous border.

3ft / 4ft

 height and spread   ✳ feature of interest   ▭▭▭ season of interest   *HERBACEOUS PERENNIALS **E—H***

HERBACEOUS PERENNIALS

HEUCHERA MICRANTHA VAR. DIVERSIFOLIA ⓩ 4–8 'PALACE PURPLE'

ALUMROOT

SAXIFRAGACEAE

This is not a particularly big plant and is perfect for the front to middle of a border. There is an increasing number of varieties that have silver markings or ruffled edges to the roundish purple leaves. The tiny flowers are held on tall airy stems.

HIERACIUM LANATUM ⓩ 5–8

WOOLLY HAWKWEED

ASTERACEAE

This is not one of the easiest plants to grow as it does not like damp conditions, but on a free-draining soil it is relatively easy. It is grown for its very attractive large felted silver leaves. The flowers are yellow daisies on tall stems and can be left or removed, depending on taste.

HOSTA 'FRANCES WILLIAMS' ⓩ 3–8

HOSTACEAE

This hosta has been included as a representative of the many variegated hostas that are available. They are all invaluable plants for the foliage garden, with their broad leaves arching outwards like a low fountain. The variegated forms are good for brightening up shady and dull positions. Grow in moist but well-drained soil with shelter from cold winds.

HOSTA SIEBOLDIANA VAR. ELEGANS ⓩ 3–8

HOSTACEAE

This hosta typifies all the non-variegated species and varieties. It has very large glaucous leaves that are strongly ribbed. It makes a very attractive ground-cover plant for either shade or sun if the soil is moist and it is sheltered from cold winds. As well as border plants, hostas make very good container plants for growing on a patio or terrace.

HOSTA 'ZOUNDS' ⓩ 3–8

HOSTACEAE

There are several hostas that have leaves with a puckered texture, much in the manner of seersucker, of which 'Zounds' is a good representative. It has large rounded leaves, up to 11in (28cm) across, and which are yellow or lime-green in color. Like all hostas, it prefers a moist soil and shelter from cold winds, and it does best in light shade.

IRIS LAEVIGATA ⓩ 4–9

IRIDACEAE

It is difficult to choose any one iris for its foliage because they are all good. However, this one has broad sword-like leaves providing a strong vertical emphasis. It grows well in shallow water and in damp soil, such as that found in a bog garden. There is a variegated form, 'Variegata', that has white stripes on the leaves. The flowers are mainly purplish-blue.

≡ leaf type   ● light preference   ⚑ speed of growth   ❀ ease of growth

IRIS PALLIDA 'VARIEGATA' ❷ 5-9
IRIDACEAE

Most of the irises have very good leaves for the foliage garden, but this one is exceptional as it retains its coloration throughout the summer. The leaves are bright green with light yellow stripes. Iris leaves are strap-shaped and held stiffly erect, making them a good contrast plant in most types of borders. This one has soft lavender flowers.

LAMIUM GALEOBDOLON ❷ 4-8
YELLOW ARCHANGEL
LAMIACEAE

An attractive plant for shady areas. The typical nettle-shaped leaves have silver markings. The flowers are yellow. It can be rampant and makes good ground cover for larger shady areas. 'Hermann's Pride' is one of the most attractive cultivars, and is less invasive than the species.

LAMIUM MACULATUM ❷ 4-8
DEADNETTLE
LAMIACEAE

This is a useful plant as it is relatively low-growing and forms a dense mat of foliage that makes good ground cover. Most varieties have some form of silver markings on them, some, such as 'White Nancy' and 'Beacon Silver' being very attractive. They have spikes of red, pink, or white flowers.

LIGULARIA DENTATA 'DESDEMONA' ❷ 4-8
LEOPARD PLANT
ASTERACEAE

The leaves on this plant are large and heart-shaped. In this form the leaves are dark green on the top and dark purple underneath. They must have a moist soil or the foliage quickly wilts. They are prey to slugs which can quickly spoil the foliage. It has orange daisy-like flowers. 'Othello' is another good form.

LOBELIA 'QUEEN VICTORIA' ❷ 4-9
CARDINAL RED LOBELIA
CAMPANULACEAE

This is a stunning plant for the foliage garden. The leaves are a deep beetroot red which are overtopped with spikes of brilliant red flowers. The plants are tall rather than wide, so you need a group to create a big impact. They look particularly good next to water. 'Bees' Flame' is similar.

LUPINUS RUSSELL HYBRIDS ❷ 4-8
LUPIN
PAPILIONACEAE

Lupins are more commonly thought of as flowering plants, but they have excellent foliage that is quite unlike any other in the garden. The leaves consist of a number of narrow pleated leaflets that radiate out from a central point. These contrast well with the simpler shapes of other plants, both before and after flowering.

---

 height and spread   ✳ feature of interest   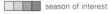 season of interest   *HERBACEOUS PERENNIALS* **H—L**

HERBACEOUS PERENNIALS

LYCHNIS CORONARIA ❷ 4–8
DUSTY MILLER
CARYOPHYLLACEAE

This is an old-fashioned cottage-garden plant with soft furry foliage that has a grayish-silver appearance. It is useful as it is a tall branched plant which few of the silvers are. The flowers are very bright magenta, although there are also more subtly colored white forms. It self-sows.

LYSIMACHIA NUMMULARIA 'AUREA' ❷ 4–8
CREEPING JENNY
PRIMULACEAE

This is a very good low ground-cover plant. It is especially useful for growing at the front of a border where it weaves among other plants, or in shady areas, such as among shrubs. The species has green leaves on long trailing stems, but in this form they are bright gold. The flowers are yellow cups.

MACLEAYA CORDATA ❷ 4–10
PLUME POPPY
PAPAVERACEAE

This is one of the few important tall perennials. It has delicately scalloped leaves that are a soft pearly gray in color. The plant has a light, airy feel about it, especially the spikes of small coral flowers. It runs and can be an invasive plant, but it looks splendid at the back of a border.

MAIANTHEMUM BIFOLIUM ❷ 4–5
MAY LILY
CONVALLARIACEAE

This is an insignificant plant, but it spreads to make very useful ground cover in shady places, especially under trees and shrubs. It is a relative of the lily of the valley. The leaves are heart-shaped, dark green, and glossy. The tiny white flowers are held on erect spikes in spring. It is invasive.

MELIANTHUS MAJOR ❷ 8–10
HONEY BUSH
MELANTHIACEAE

Although this is often treated as an annual it is a perennial and will survive all but a severe winter outside. Although it does have spikes of chocolate-red flowers, it is grown for its large silver leaves, which are subdivided toothed leaflets, making this very much a plant to catch the eye.

MELISSA OFFICINALIS 'AUREA' ❷ 3–7
LEMON BALM
LAMIACEAE

The species is commonly grown as a culinary herb. This form is similar except that the small nettle-shaped leaves are splashed with gold. Whereas the species prefers sun, this does best in light shade, where it will often illuminate the gloom. It seeds vigorously, so cut back the flowering stems.

 leaf type   light preference   🌱 speed of growth   ease of growth

MENTHA REQUIENII ❷ 6–9
CORSICAN MINT
LAMIACEAE

This is a very low carpeting plant that follows the contours of all that it covers. The leaves are round and their very small size is made up for by the quantity produced. They are very fragrant, with a typical mint smell when crushed. The lilac flowers are also very small. It must have a lightly shaded, moist position.

⅛in
6ft+

MONARDA DIDYMA ❷ 4–9
BERGAMOT
LAMIACEAE

The great attraction of the foliage of this plant is not so much its appearance as its wonderful fragrance when crushed. It only needs the slightest touch to release it. The flowers are borne in whorls and are either bright red or pink. This plant must have a rich and moist soil and needs to be replanted every few years.

3ft
18in

MORINA LONGIFOLIA ❷ 6–9
WHORLFLOWER
MORINACEAE

This is not the easiest of plants to grow, but it is worth the effort for its long glossy leaves that resemble those of many thistles. It is not a thistle, however, and has drooping tubular white and pink flowers arranged in whorls. It needs a well-drained soil, especially during winter, and a sunny position.

3ft
12in

NEPETA X FAASSENII ❷ 4–8
CATMINT
LAMIACEAE

Most of the catmints are worth growing for their foliage, especially the gray ones such as this. The foliage acts as a perfect foil for the misty blue flowers and also for any pastel colors on adjacent plants. The leaves also have the advantage of being fragrant. After flowering, cut the plant to the ground.

18in
2ft

NYMPHAEA SPECIES AND CULTIVARS ❷ 4–11
WATER LILY
NYMPHAEACEAE

These plants like deep water and are extremely useful foliage plants for such positions. The leaves are glossy and round, varying in size according to species and variety. They can be used in anything from tubs to lakes. Most spread quite quickly and may need culling regularly.

6in
6ft

ORIGANUM VULGARE 'AUREUM' ❷ 5–9
GOLDEN MARJORAM
LAMIACEAE

Although this is frequently used as a herb it also makes a very good foliage plant. It forms a rounded hummock with small golden leaves which in some clones turn green as the season progresses. The purple flowers spoil the effect so they should be removed, especially as they can self-sow everywhere.

18in
18in

---

 height and spread   ✳ feature of interest   ▭ season of interest   *HERBACEOUS PERENNIALS L—O*

HERBACEOUS PERENNIALS

PERSICARIA AFFINIS ❷ 3–8
POLYGONACEAE

An excellent foliage plant that is especially useful for ground cover. The foliage has a fresh look about it in spring, and takes on a reddish and finally brown tinge in autumn. It forms a dense mat, but is not invasive as it is easily controlled. The attractive pink flower spikes also turn red and brown in autumn. It grows best in a moist soil.

PERSICARIA BISTORTA ❷ 4–8
BISTORT
POLYGONACEAE

This plant is a little like *P. affinis*, except it is on a larger scale. The leaves are not so leathery and do not change color over the season, but they make attractive ground cover and set off the spikes of pink flowers beautifully. It needs a moist soil, and does well in either sun or light shade.

PETASITES JAPONICUS ❷ 5–9
BUTTERBUR
ASTERACEAE

This is a plant that is definitely only for the larger garden. It can form spectacular sheets of ground cover, with its large, up to 5ft (1.5m) wide, leaves. They are round and held up to 7ft (2m) above the ground in some varieties. This is a plant to grow in large drifts through damp woods.

PHLOX PANICULATA 'NORAH LEIGH' ❷ 4–8
POLEMONIACEAE

Border phlox are not generally thought of as foliage plants, but this variety, as well as several others such as 'Harlequin' and 'Pink Posie' are frequently grown for their variegated leaves. 'Norah Leigh' has very distinct splashes of ivory on the leaves and also produces lilac flowers. This plant grows best in a fertile, moist soil in full sun or partial shade.

PHORMIUM TENAX ❷ 9–10
NEW ZEALAND FLAX
AGAVACEAE

Although technically a shrub, this is usually grown as a perennial by gardeners. It forms a very large plant with great strap-like leaves that stiffly radiate out. The species has pale green leaves but there are numerous colored and variegated cultivars. It makes a spectacular specimen plant when mature.

PHUOPSIS STYLOSA ❷ 5–8
RUBIACEAE

Perhaps not the first plant to think of in terms of foliage, but it has whorls of narrow leaves that form a useful contrast to other types of foliage. It is a spreading plant that scrambles around and through other plants. It has spheres of attractive pink flowers. The foliage is scented, especially after rain. It prefers a moist but well-drained, gritty soil.

🌿 leaf type   ● light preference   ⚘ speed of growth   ❀ ease of growth

PLANTAGO MAJOR 'RUBRIFOLIA' ❷6–7

GIANT PLANTAIN

PLANTAGINACEAE

While the species is the bane of any lawn, the purple-leaf form makes a good foliage plant. The leaves are quite large and ribbed. They are slightly coarse and so the plant should not be put in a prime site, but none the less it definitely has its uses. It does not spread as vigorously as its weedy parent.

PULMONARIA SACCHARATA ❷4–8

LUNGWORT

BORAGINACEAE

There are several lungworts that make excellent foliage plants. They have rough-textured leaves that are often spotted or splashed with silver. Once the flowering is over in spring, they should be sheared over and the new foliage will remain fresh for the rest of the year. It is good for shade.

RANUNCULUS FLUITANS ❷5–9

WATER BUTTERCUP

RANUNCULACEAE

This is not a common garden plant, but is often seen in the wild. It is one of the few good foliage plants for flowing water, such as a stream. The leaves are very fine and wave in the current of passing water like long tresses of hair. They are complemented with white buttercup-like flowers.

RHEUM PALMATUM ❷5–9

ORNAMENTAL RHUBARB

POLYGONACEAE

This is a spectacular plant for the foliage garden. It looks like rhubarb, but it is on a larger scale with less fleshy leaves that have jagged or deep-cut edges. They are usually reddish, with varieties such as 'Atropurpureum' being dark red. They make good feature plants, especially in a mixed border.

RODGERSIA PINNATA ❷5–8

SAXIFRAGACEAE

Like the other rodgersias, this one has good foliage. It has large leaves made up of a number of leaflets. The leaves are heavily veined, creating an interesting texture, especially as they are glossy and reflect the light. They also have large spikes of cream or pink flowers. To do well, they need a moist soil and preferably shelter from cold winds.

RODGERSIA PODOPHYLLA ❷5–8

SAXIFRAGACEAE

Most of the rodgersias have handsome foliage. This one has large palmate leaves that have a tint of bronze on their textured surfaces. They do best in light shade, or sun where the soil is moist, and need to be sheltered from cold winds. Either way, a shaft of sun on the leaves can be stunning. *R. aesculifolia* is another good species.

↕ height and spread   ✳ feature of interest   ▭ season of interest   *HERBACEOUS PERENNIALS* **P—R**

HERBACEOUS PERENNIALS

SEDUM SPECTABILE ⓩ 4–10
ICE PLANT
CRASSULACEAE

Although mainly grown for their autumn flowers this species and its cultivars and hybrids also make excellent foliage plants for most of the spring and summer. The fleshy leaves have a glaucous gray tinge to them, making them look almost icy (hence the name). It makes a good foil for most other plants.

SEDUM TELEPHIUM SUBSP. MAXIMUM 'ATROPURPUREUM' ⓩ 4–9
ORPINE
CRASSULACEAE

Sedum telephium has produced many good forms for the foliage garden. The purple ones are the most useful. 'Atropurpureum' has very dark purple leaves, almost brown in some lights. 'Mohrchen' is a new and excellent cultivar.

SEDUM 'VERA JAMESON' ⓩ 4–9
CRASSULACEAE

This is a much smaller sedum than the previous one, but again it is noted for its beautiful purple foliage that lasts throughout the summer and autumn. It makes an excellent front-of-border plant. 'Bertram Anderson' is another plant suitable for a similar position, but 'Vera Jameson' has a more steely-blue tinge to its purple foliage: an unusual and useful color.

SELINUM WALLICHIANUM ⓩ 8–10
APIACEAE

Also known as *S. tenuifolium*, this is a delightful member of the cow parsley family, with wonderful lacy foliage that is very delicately cut. This contrasts well with the large flat heads of white flowers. Whereas cow parsley is for the wild garden, this works well in more formal borders. It requires a moderately fertile, moist but well-drained soil.

SILENE UNIFLORA 'DRUETT'S VARIEGATED' ⓩ 3–7
VARIEGATED SEA CAMPION
CARYOPHYLLACEAE

Also known as *S. maritima*, this is a very attractive variegated plant for the rock garden or front of a border. It is a low-growing mat-forming plant with small grayish-green leaves, which in the variegated form are splashed with creamy-yellow. The flowers are white and have an inflated calyx.

SISYRINCHIUM STRIATUM 'AUNT MAY' ⓩ 7–8
IRIDACEAE

S. striatum itself can be a useful plant with its fans of stiff sword-like leaves. However, they have a habit of blackening at the tips which spoils their appearance. 'Aunt May' is a more appealing plant, with grayish-green leaves striped with cream. Unfortunately it is not very robust and needs replacing regularly. It dislikes excessive winter wet.

| leaf type | light preference | speed of growth | ease of growth |

STACHYS BYZANTINA ❷4–8
LAMB'S EARS
LAMIACEAE

One of the most valuable of all foliage plants. It has furry leaves that are silver-gray. It forms large mats which are invaluable at the front of borders and will go with most colors. Some gardeners like to remove the flowering stems with their pink flowers. It can look sad in wet conditions.

TANACETUM PARTHENIUM 'AUREUM' ❷4–9
GOLDEN FEVERFEW
ASTERACEAE

This is a delicate bushy plant with chrysanthemum-type foliage, which in this variety is golden yellow. Although a true perennial it is often better grown for only one or two years, as the foliage is then fresher and more concentrated. It has small white daisy flowers that seed everywhere.

TANACETUM VULGARE 'SILVER LACE' ❷4–8
TANSY
ASTERACEAE

Tanacetum vulgare runs and can be a bit of a nuisance so is best avoided in smaller gardens. However, its variety 'Silver Lace' can be so beautiful it is worth trying to contain it. The finely cut leaves are splashed with silver, which is particularly noticeable in spring. It is a useful upright foliage plant.

TYPHA LATIFOLIA ❷3–11
REED MACE
TYPHACEAE

These are aquatic plants that grow in shallow water. They produce slightly arching stiff sword-like leaves which look particularly effective when used en masse in a pond. It is a rampant plant that is only suitable for larger ponds and even here it needs to be kept under control.

VALERIANA PHU 'AUREA' ❷5–9
VALERIANACEAE

The species has no garden value at all, but this variety, 'Aurea', has good golden foliage in spring that turns to lime-green in summer. It stands out well in spring when there is little else of similar coloring around. The flowers are dirty white and are usually removed as they do nothing for the appearance of the plant. It prefers moist soil.

VERATRUM NIGRUM ❷6–9
MELANTHIACEAE

This is a truly splendid foliage plant. It produces wonderful clumps of light green pleated leaves, somewhat reminiscent of hostas. Unfortunately it falls prey to slugs, so these must be controlled. It also has spectacular flower stems which take at least seven years to appear. It is a woodland plant, and prefers moist but well-drained soil.

 height and spread   ✱ feature of interest    season of interest   *HERBACEOUS PERENNIALS* **S—V**

GRASSES

ALOPECURUS PRATENSIS 'AUREOVARIEGATUS' ❷ 5–8
VARIEGATED FOX TAIL
POACEAE

This is one of the best of the variegated grasses in that it has leaves that are very brightly colored with golden stripes. The flowers are not particularly attractive, and they can be removed. It is an easy plant that can be used to create a splash of color either in a mixed or grass border.

ARUNDO DONAX ❷ 6–10
GIANT REED
POACEAE

This is an enormous plant that towers above other vegetation. It will soon produce a grove of tall stems with wide drooping mid-green leaves. There is a variegated form, 'Versicolor', which has cream-striped foliage, and is shorter than the species. However, it is frost tender and best grown in a container.

BRIZA MEDIA ❷ 4–10
QUAKING GRASS
POACEAE

This is a perennial quaking grass, so called because the locket-shaped flower heads are constantly quivering. The foliage forms in loose tufts and with individual narrow flat leaves. They are not spectacular but make a good foil for the flowers. It does well on poor, dry soils.

CAREX BUCHANANII ❷ 6–9
LEATHER LEAF SEDGE
CYPERACEAE

This is a valuable plant because the leaves are a rufous brown, an unusual color for foliage. The leaves are nearly cylindrical and have a distinctive curl at the tips. The general effect is of a fountain of brown. The color is best maintained if the plant is grown in full sun, where it prefers a damp soil.

CAREX ELATA 'AUREA' ❷ 5–9
BOWLES GOLDEN SEDGE
CYPERACEAE

A large tufted sedge with bright yellow-gold leaves with green margins. A light shade will preserve the color. In deep shade it will revert to green. It is also known as *C. stricta* 'Bowles Golden' and *C. riparia* 'Bowles Golden'. It needs a moist soil and does well next to ponds.

CAREX OSHIMENSIS 'EVERGOLD' ❷ 6–9
CYPERACEAE

Also known as *C. morrowii*, this is a popular sedge with a tufted habit and a distinctive yellow stripe down the center of each leaf. There is also a white-striped version 'Variegata'. It produces insignificant flowers on triangular stems which can be removed. It the wild it grows in damp woodlands, and prefers a fertile, moist, but well-drained soil.

≋ leaf type | ● light preference | ⚘ speed of growth | ✿ ease of growth

CORTADERIA SELLOANA ⓩ 7–10
PAMPAS GRASS
POACEAE

Tall-growing grass forming large spreading clumps with graceful arching leaves and tall stems of feathery flowers. The leaves are very sharp-edged and can cause deep cuts. There are several cultivars with different-sized plants, as well as the variegated forms 'Aureolineata' and 'Albolineata'.

8ft / 7ft

DESCHAMPSIA CESPITOSA 'GOLDGEHÄNGE' ⓩ 5–9
TUFTED HAIR GRASS
POACEAE

Like many grasses, this one is grown mainly for the effect of its flower and seed heads, but the foliage helps to give them a much longer season of interest. This one has a cloud of golden flowers. It is also known as 'Golden Shower' and 'Golden Veil'. It can seed itself around the garden.

3ft / 3ft

ELYMUS MAGELLANICUS ⓩ 7–8
POACEAE

Also known as *Agropyron magellanicum*, this is one of the best of the really blue grasses. It has rather broad lax leaves that grow in a loose tuft. They are a less intense color in the winter. The insignificant flowers appear throughout the summer. It is related to the invasive *E. repens* (couch grass), but is easily controlled.

6in / 12in

FESTUCA GLAUCA ⓩ 4–8
BLUE FESCUE
POACEAE

This is another plant with blue leaves, although a little greener than the previous one. The leaves are narrow. It develops a more intense color on dry soils. The plant itself is a dense, rounded clump. The flowers are of little importance. 'Blaufuchs' is the best of the cultivars.

8in / 8in

HAKONECHLOA MACRA 'AUREOLA' ⓩ 5–9
HAKONE GRASS
POACEAE

A clump-forming grass with broad leaves that loosely arch. In this cultivar the leaves are yellow with green stripes. As the leaves age, they take on a reddish-brown glow. It is a slow-growing plant, and although best in a border it makes a good container plant. There are other interesting cultivars.

12in / 12in

HORDEUM JUBATUM ⓩ 4–8
SQUIRRELTAIL GRASS
POACEAE

This is an annual grass, although sometimes treated as a short-lived perennial. It is mainly grown for the arching silky plumes of flowers that it produces. These mix well with a large number of plants including annual bedding plants. It seeds itself vigorously, providing plenty of replacements.

18in / 12in

 height and spread   ✳ feature of interest   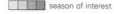 season of interest   *GRASSES A–H*

GRASSES

LAGURUS OVATUS ❷ 2–11
HARE'S TAIL GRASS
POACEAE

This is an annual grass that is primarily grown for its flower heads. It is a tufted plant with dense oval heads of soft white flowers, a bit like small powder puffs. These appear over pale green soft flat long leaves. There is a dwarf form called 'Nanus'. Sow the seeds where they are to grow.

LUZULA SYLVATICA ❷ 5–9
GREATER WOODRUSH
JUNCACEAE

An untidy sprawling plant. It spreads by rhizomes to make very effective ground cover. It is valuable in that it is one of the few grasses that will tolerate dry shade. The leaves are shiny green and there are several varieties, of which 'Marginata' with its white edges is one of the best.

MILIUM EFFUSUM 'AUREUM' ❷ 6–9
BOWLES GOLDEN GRASS
POACEAE

This is one of the great grasses for the foliage gardener. It starts to grow early in the spring with leaves that are a very soft yellow. The rest of the plant is a similar color. It prefers light shade but will turn green if the conditions are too shady. It is wonderful for lighting up a shady spot.

MISCANTHUS SINENSIS ❷ 4–9
EULALIA
POACEAE

Miscanthus is becoming one of the most developed of garden grasses with many species and cultivars now available. They are all attractive both for their foliage and tall flowering stems. The leaves are long and arching, some narrow and others wider. Most are plain green but there are also variegated ones.

MOLINIA CAERULEA ❷ 5–9
PURPLE MOOR GRASS
POACEAE

A species of grass with many good cultivars. It is a medium-height tufted grass, with narrow green leaves. The purple in the name comes from the color of the flower heads. It is good for acid soils. The form 'Variegata', shown here, is one of the most popular, and the easiest to grow.

PANICUM VIRGATUM ❷ 5–9
SWITCH GRASS
POACEAE

This is a moderately tall, upright plant that has airy heads of small flowers. From the foliage gardener's point of view, it is important for its green leaves that are tinged red. This intensifies as the season progresses, so that in some cultivars the plant is really ablaze by autumn. 'Hänse Herms' is one of the best.

🌿 leaf type   ⬤ light preference   ⚘ speed of growth   ⚙ ease of growth

PENNISETUM VILLOSUM ❷ 9–10

FEATHER TOP

POACEAE

This is a very decorative plant grown for its flower heads. The dark green foliage is in a loose clump and creates a background plant, but not much more. The flowers are like delicate bottle brushes held on long slightly arching stems. The plant is also sometimes known as *P. longistylum*.

18in / 18in

PHALARIS ARUNDINACEA VAR. PICTA ❷ 4–9

GARDENER'S GARTERS

POACEAE

This is a very attractive grass, but unfortunately it is also a very active one and can become invasive. The leaves are somewhat drooping but have a very fresh appearance with pale green leaves striped with white and flushed with pink when new. It does need confining in some way.

3ft / 6ft+

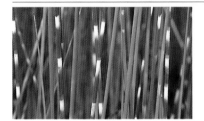

SCHOENOPLECTUS LACUSTRIS SUBSP.
TABERNAEMONTANI 'ZEBRINUS' ❷ 4–8

CLUB RUSH

CYPERACEAE

Still often known as *Scirpus*, this is an attractive rush for growing in shallow water or in the damp soil of a bog garden. Its stems are gray-green with horizontal bands around them of a creamy yellow. It forms a spreading clump.

3ft / 3ft

STIPA GIGANTEA ❷ 8–10

GOLDEN OATS

POACEAE

This is a very popular grass, mainly because of its tall flowering stems that carry airy sprays of golden flowers. It is a clump-forming plant with evergreen leaves which are narrow. They are not individually conspicuous but work as a tufted clump and make good ground cover for an open border.

6ft / 3ft

UNCINIA UNCINATA RUBRA ❷ 8–11

CYPERACEAE

This plant has become popular with foliage gardeners because of its unusual leaves. They are deep red which contrasts beautifully with the underlying bright green. It works well as a small accent plant or in a group. There is a similarly named species *Uncinia rubra*, which is very similar in appearance but larger overall. It prefers a moist but well-drained soil.

12in / 10in

ZEA MAYS ❷ 3–11

MAIZE

POACEAE

This is an annual grass that is also seen in the vegetable garden. It is a tall erect plant with wide drooping leaves. A clump at the back of a border can be very impressive. There are several purely ornamental varieties with variegated foliage, including white, yellow, and pink variegations.

7ft / 18in

---

 height and spread   ✱ feature of interest   ▭▭▭ season of interest   *GRASSES* **L–Z**

BAMBOOS

BAMBUSA MULTIPLEX ⓩ 8–10
HEDGE BAMBOO
POACEAE

A tender bamboo that can be grown in frost-free areas. It can grow very tall and, as its common name suggests, can be used as a hedging bamboo. It has long narrow leaves. In colder areas, it can be grown in containers and moved outside in the summer. The variety 'Fernleaf' has fern-like foliage.

CHUSQUEA CULEOU ⓩ 8–11
POACEAE

A beautiful bamboo with papery leaf sheaths that contrast with the shiny green stems, creating a striped effect. The leaves are narrow and willow-like. The lower parts of the canes take on a bristly effect as the leaf-stalks remain after the lower leaves have finished their useful life and have fallen. Grow in a moist but well-drained soil and shelter from cold winds.

PHYLLOSTACHYS BAMBUSOIDES ⓩ 7–10
GIANT TIMBER BAMBOO
POACEAE

As its common name suggests, this is a tall bamboo. It spreads to form a large clump and makes a good thicket. The canes are shiny green and bear long wide leaves that are colored dark green. There are several forms, some of which have yellow or striped canes. It prefers a moist, well-drained soil.

PHYLLOSTACHYS FLEXUOSA ⓩ 6–10
ZIGZAG BAMBOO
POACEAE

This bamboo derives its common name from the fact that the ribbed stems are not straight but slightly zigzagged, changing direction just below each leaf node. They are green, turning to black, and they are often very tall. The narrow leaves are up to 6in (15cm) long, and retain their fresh color throughout winter.

PHYLLOSTACHYS NIGRA ⓩ 7–10
BLACK BAMBOO
POACEAE

This bamboo is named after the way its green stems change to shiny black in their second and subsequent years. The stems have an arching habit. The leaves are lance-shaped and dark green. There are some varieties in which the canes turn yellow instead of black. Grow in a moist but well-drained soil.

PLEIOBLASTUS AURICOMUS ⓩ 7–11
POACEAE

This is a slow-spreading bamboo with very attractive variegated foliage. It has purple stems that bear yellow leaves that are striped with green. It is a useful plant for a shrub border. It is also known as *P. viridistriatus, Arundinaria auricoma,* and *A. viridistriata.* This bamboo should be grown in a moist but well-drained soil, and sheltered from cold winds.

≣ leaf type　　　● light preference　　　⚘ speed of growth　　　✿ ease of growth

PLEIOBLASTUS VARIEGATUS ❷ 7–11
DWARF WHITE-STRIPED BAMBOO
POACEAE

Also known as *Arundinaria fortunei* and *A. variegata*, this is an attractive variegated bamboo with creamy-white stripes down the length of its long dark leaves. The canes are pale green. It is neither tall nor invasive, making this a very attractive plant for the smaller garden. It prefers a moist soil.

30in / 4ft

PSEUDOSASA JAPONICA ❷ 7–10
ARROW BAMBOO
POACEAE

This is one of the commonest of the garden bamboos. Although it is quite coarse, it is worth its place as it is tough and creates good protection for other plants. It forms spreading clumps of green stems, with persistent brown sheaths. The foliage is broad, pointed, and evergreen. Grow in a moist soil.

16ft / 10ft

SASA VEITCHII ❷ 6–10
KUMA ZASA
POACEAE

This bamboo is medium-sized, and known for its variegated foliage during the winter months when the dark green leaves take on distinctive off-white margins. It is a hardy evergreen with pale stems and purple sheaths. Unfortunately, it can be invasive. It prefers a moist, well-drained soil.

5ft / 10ft

SEMIARUNDINARIA FASTUOSA ❷ 6–9
NARIHIRA BAMBOO
POACEAE

This bamboo forms dense spreading clumps. It is tall and upright, and is useful for screens and backdrops. The attractive stems are green striped with purple, and when the papery cane sheaths open the cane is dark purple underneath. The lower part of the canes is often bare. Leaves are up to 6in (15cm) long.

23ft / 7ft

SHIBATAEA KUMASASA ❷ 6–10
POACEAE

This is a low-growing evergreen bamboo which has the advantage that it does not spread invasively. The canes are short-jointed and brownish-green in color. The leaves are deep green, relatively broad and long, making a good display. It is an excellent bamboo for smaller gardens. It needs a moist but well-drained soil in sun or partial shade.

6in / 2ft

YUSHANIA ANCEPS ❷ 8–10
ANCEPS BAMBOO
POACEAE

Also known as *Arundinacea anceps*, this is an attractive but invasive bamboo, which will throw up new clumps some distance from the original plant. The stems are tall and gracefully arching. The pointed leaves are glossy and mid-green in color. Grow in a moist but well-drained soil.

13ft / 10ft

---

 height and spread   ✻ feature of interest   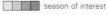 season of interest   *BAMBOOS* **B—Y**

FERNS

ADIANTUM PEDATUM Ⓩ 3-8
NORTHERN MAIDENHAIR FERN
ADIANTACEAE

A very attractive fern for a choice position. It has slender strap-like fronds that are divided to the central rib. The stems are black and the fronds a fresh mid-green. Together they make a delicate plant, especially in spring when the new leaves are uncoiling. Increase by division or from spores.

18in / 12in

ADIANTUM VENUSTUM Ⓩ 5-8
KASHMIR MAIDENHAIR FERN
ADIANTACEAE

A very beautiful fern with each frond made up of hundreds of tiny triangular leaflets. Each frond droops over its neighbour in a very attractive way, almost like a waterfall. In fact it grows well and looks good next to a waterfall or a shady water feature. It needs a moist soil and can be increased by spores.

12in / 12in

ASPLENIUM NIDUS Ⓩ 2-11
BIRD'S-NEST FERN
ASPLENIACEAE

The name of this fern is well chosen as the leaves spread out like a shuttlecock, producing an open-centered plant. The fronds are whole and are broad and lance-shaped. They are a glossy pale green with a contrasting brown-black central vein. They are tender plants and best grown in containers.

3ft / 2ft

ASPLENIUM SCOLOPENDRIUM Ⓩ 6-8
HART'S-TONGUE FERN
ASPLENIACEAE

Unlike most ferns, this has undivided mid-green fronds. They are like a broad undulating tongue, ending in a point. There are a number of cultivars, some, especially the Crispum Group, with very attractive curled edges. They make a good contrast to the more frilly foliage. Increase by division or from spores.

18in / 18in

ASPLENIUM TRICHOMANES Ⓩ 5-8
MAIDENHAIR SPLEENWORT
ASPLENIACEAE

This is an attractive species of asplenium with long slightly tapering fronds, each made up of leathery rounded-oblong leaflets. They are bright green with glossy black or brown midribs. Not being lacy like other ferns means this provides a good contrast. Increase from spores.

9in / 12in

ATHYRIUM FILIX-FEMINA Ⓩ 4-9
LADY FERN
WOODSIACEAE

The lady fern has beautiful much-divided fronds which arch in a graceful manner. They are a fresh light green. It should not be crowded so that it can show off its shape. There are many cultivars with differing frond shapes. Increase by division or from spores. It self-sows, but rarely becomes a nuisance.

2ft / 2ft

SPRING SUMMER AUTUMN WINTER

▦ leaf type   ● light preference   ♟ speed of growth   ✿ ease of growth

ATHYRIUM NIPONICUM ❷ 5–8
PAINTED FERN
WOODSIACEAE
This is a very beautiful small fern and is well worth its place in any garden. It gets its name because the grayish fronds are "painted" with a delicate flush of red. The stalks are also a deep red. *A.n.* var. *pictum* is the best-colored form. The fronds are lacy and triangular in shape. Increase by division.

12in / 12in

BLECHNUM PENNA-MARINA ❷ 10–11
BLECHNACEAE
A delicate fern with slender fronds of two types. The sterile outer ones are long and narrow with a sparse covering of narrow pinnae (leaflets). The inner ones are shorter and cut to the central rib. It is a spreading plant, making good ground cover for a shady rock garden. This fern requires a moist, acid soil in order to thrive. Increase from spores.

12in / 2ft

BLECHNUM SPICANT ❷ 5–8
HARD FERN
BLECHNACEAE
This is a very hardy fern that is useful for damp places with a peaty soil. It forms small clumps from which erupt narrow fronds with deep indentations. They are leathery and dark green in color. There are a number of interesting cultivars to try. Increase by division or from spores.

18in / 12in

CYRTOMIUM FALCATUM ❷ 6–10
JAPANESE HOLLY FERN
DRYOPTERIDACEAE
An intriguing fern with broad leaflets that look very much as if they are the holly leaves of its name. They are arranged alternately on the stems of the frond and are a shiny dark green. This plant is not completely hardy and is only suitable for warmer areas. Increase either from spores or by division.

18in / 12in

DICKSONIA ANTARCTICA ❷ 9–10
AUSTRALIAN TREE FERN
DICKSONIACEAE
This is a remarkable foliage plant, part tree, part fern. It starts as a fern but as it discards older leaves so the base grows to provide new ones, until eventually it forms a tree-like trunk with the fronds held high. The fronds are large but deeply cut and delicate. Increase from spores.

4in / 13ft

DRYOPTERIS DILATATA ❷ 5–8
BROAD BUCKLER FERN
DRYOPTERIDACEAE
Also known as *D. austriaca*, this is an attractive arching fern with broad much-divided fronds. The pinnae (leaflets) are dark green and roughly triangular in shape. The stems are dark brown. There are several cultivars with crests or crisped margins. It can be increased either from spores or by division.

2ft / 2ft

⬍ height and spread   ✳ feature of interest   ▢▢▢ season of interest   *FERNS **A—D***

FERNS

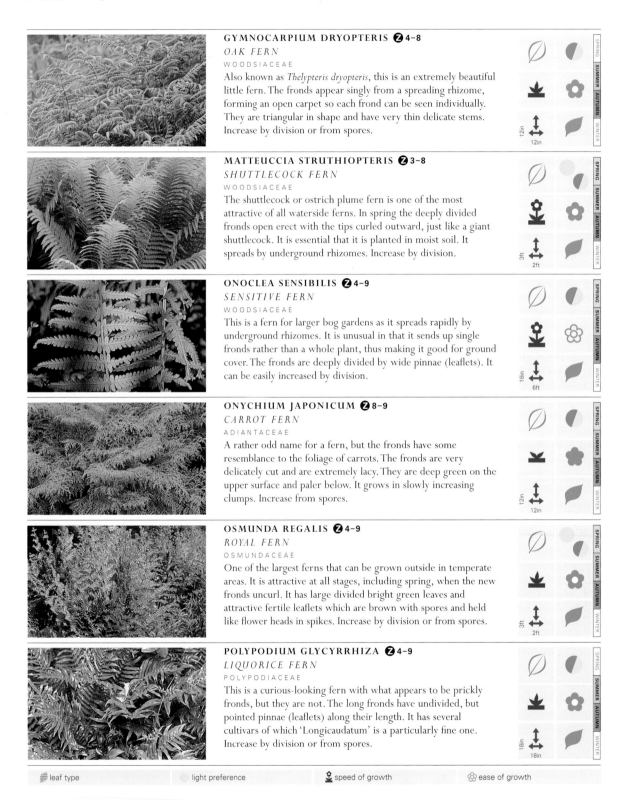

GYMNOCARPIUM DRYOPTERIS Z 4–8

OAK FERN

WOODSIACEAE

Also known as *Thelypteris dryopteris*, this is an extremely beautiful little fern. The fronds appear singly from a spreading rhizome, forming an open carpet so each frond can be seen individually. They are triangular in shape and have very thin delicate stems. Increase by division or from spores.

MATTEUCCIA STRUTHIOPTERIS Z 3–8

SHUTTLECOCK FERN

WOODSIACEAE

The shuttlecock or ostrich plume fern is one of the most attractive of all waterside ferns. In spring the deeply divided fronds open erect with the tips curled outward, just like a giant shuttlecock. It is essential that it is planted in moist soil. It spreads by underground rhizomes. Increase by division.

ONOCLEA SENSIBILIS Z 4–9

SENSITIVE FERN

WOODSIACEAE

This is a fern for larger bog gardens as it spreads rapidly by underground rhizomes. It is unusual in that it sends up single fronds rather than a whole plant, thus making it good for ground cover. The fronds are deeply divided by wide pinnae (leaflets). It can be easily increased by division.

ONYCHIUM JAPONICUM Z 8–9

CARROT FERN

ADIANTACEAE

A rather odd name for a fern, but the fronds have some resemblance to the foliage of carrots. The fronds are very delicately cut and are extremely lacy. They are deep green on the upper surface and paler below. It grows in slowly increasing clumps. Increase from spores.

OSMUNDA REGALIS Z 4–9

ROYAL FERN

OSMUNDACEAE

One of the largest ferns that can be grown outside in temperate areas. It is attractive at all stages, including spring, when the new fronds uncurl. It has large divided bright green leaves and attractive fertile leaflets which are brown with spores and held like flower heads in spikes. Increase by division or from spores.

POLYPODIUM GLYCYRRHIZA Z 4–9

LIQUORICE FERN

POLYPODIACEAE

This is a curious-looking fern with what appears to be prickly fronds, but they are not. The long fronds have undivided, but pointed pinnae (leaflets) along their length. It has several cultivars of which 'Longicaudatum' is a particularly fine one. Increase by division or from spores.

leaf type   light preference   speed of growth   ease of growth

POLYPODIUM VULGARE ❷6-8
COMMON POLYPODY
POLYPODIACEAE

A common garden fern with many interesting cultivars for the foliage gardener to explore. It quickly spreads to form a good colony which makes effective ground cover. It has deeply cut leaves, but the form 'Cornubiense' provides a more lacy effect. Increase by division or from spores.

POLYSTICHUM ACULEATUM ❷3-6
HARD SHIELD FERN
DRYOPTERIDACEAE

This is a very elegant fern with long arching fronds. They are broadly lance-shaped and deeply cut. Their color is yellow-green in spring, becoming a darker, shiny green as they mature. It needs a moist soil in order to thrive. Increase by division or from spores.

POLYSTICHUM MUNITUM ❷3-8
GIANT HOLLY FERN
DRYOPTERIDACEAE

This is a very beautiful fern. It forms large clumps of long erect but arching fronds. They are lance-shaped with a leathery texture and a dark green color. The pinnae (leaflets) have spines, hence its name. It is also known as the Christmas fern or the sword fern. Increase from spores.

POLYSTICHUM SETIFERUM ❷6-9
SOFT SHIELD FERN
DRYOPTERIDACEAE

The soft shield fern is a very graceful and beautiful plant with much-divided fronds. The general shape is spear-shaped and the color a soft mid-green. The stems are covered with shaggy brown scales. This is a good plant for a dry bank. It can be increased either by division or from spores.

THELYPTERIS PALUSTRIS ❷5-8
MARSH FERN
THELYPTERIDACEAE

Also known as *Dryopteris thelypteris*, this is a creeping fern that spreads by black rhizomes. It has typical fern-like lacy foliage that is deeply cut. The color is a pale green. It grows well in boggy ground and is useful for growing near and even in water. Increase by division or from spores.

WOODWARDIA RADICANS ❷8-9
CHAIN FERN
BLECHNACEAE

The chain fern is a wonderful sight with graceful arching stems of divided leaves. The name comes from the chains of spores to be found on the backs of the pinnae (leaflets). It is slightly tender and therefore needs some winter protection in colder parts. It can be increased by pegging down the bud at the tip of the fronds.

 height and spread   feature of interest   season of interest   *FERNS* **G—W**

93

TREES AND SHRUBS

ABIES KOREANA 🅩 5-6
KOREAN FIR
PINACEAE
A very beautiful slow-growing pine with a fine open conical shape, the symmetry of which is maintained as the tree grows. The foliage is dark green above and silver below, with the spring growth being silver all over. The cones, which appear at an early age, are a most beautiful violet-purple color.

ACER NEGUNDO 'FLAMINGO' 🅩 5-8
BOX MAPLE
ACERACEAE
Acer negundo is a small tree or a bush if pollarded. This makes it suitable for a small garden. The attractive aspect of 'Flamingo' is the fresh-looking pale pink variegation to the new leaves, making it a valuable foliage plant. 'Variegatum' is another good form, this time with white variegations.

ACER PALMATUM 🅩 6-8
JAPANESE MAPLE
ACERACEAE
Acer palmatum is very attractive in its own right with its palmate leaves with pointed lobes. However, it is its many cultivars that are mainly of interest. Some, such as 'Atropurpureum' have rich red foliage, while others such as 'Dissectum' have very attractive deeply cut leaves. Most have good autumn color.

ACER SHIRASAWANUM 'AUREUM' 🅩 5-7
GOLDEN JAPANESE MAPLE
ACERACEAE
There are several interesting Japanese maples, but for the foliage gardener this is one of the best. It forms a large rounded bush and is covered with pale yellow leaves. These are lobed like most maples. Other forms have much more dissected leaves. It is slow-growing and suitable for large rock gardens.

ALOYSIA TRIPHYLLA 🅩 8-11
LEMON VERBENA
VERBENACEAE
This is a deciduous shrub grown for its very fragrant foliage. When crushed, the leaves emit a strong smell of lemon. The leaves are narrow and willow-like. It is not completely hardy, and since it makes a good container plant it is best overwintered inside and brought out for the warmer months.

AUCUBA JAPONICA 'VARIEGATA' 🅩 6-10
SPOTTED LAUREL
AUCUBACEAE
Aucuba is a plant to love or hate. It can be overpowering, especially in small gardens, but it has some advantages, especially in dry shady situations. There are several other variegated forms, such as 'Crotonifolia', which have spotted or splashed leaves that lighten the bush considerably.

≣ leaf type   ● light preference   ⚲ speed of growth   ❀ ease of growth

BERBERIS THUNBERGII F. ATROPURPUREA ⓩ 5–8
COMMON BARBERRY
BERBERIDACEAE

There are so many good barberries for the foliage gardener to explore it is difficult to single one out. However, *B. thunbergii*, although common, still has a place, especially in its form *B.t.f. atropurpurea* with purple foliage. Another is 'Rose Glow' which has purple leaves splashed with pink.

BETULA PENDULA ⓩ 2–7
SILVER BIRCH
BETULACEAE

A small tree that is suitable for the small garden. It has silver bark and small, trembling leaves that create a pleasant dappled shade on pendulous branches. There are plenty of cultivars and other species which are all variations on the same theme. Some have a more weeping habit; others have whiter bark.

BUXUS SEMPERVIRENS ⓩ 6–8
BOX
BUXACEAE

Box is one of the foliage gardener's most-used plants. It reigns supreme for low hedging and topiary. Its small shiny leaves and compact nature mean it is easy to trim or shape. The dwarf form 'Suffruticosa' is the best for miniature hedges. There are also variegated as well as plain-leaved forms.

CAMELLIA JAPONICA ⓩ 7–8
THEACEAE

One immediately associates camellias with their beautiful flowers but they also have extremely good all-year-round foliage. The leaves are quite large and usually a glossy dark green. The gloss means that they are useful for lighting up dark corners. Any of the hundreds of cultivars are suitable. Camellias require a moist but well-drained, acid soil.

CEANOTHUS IMPRESSUS ⓩ 8–10
CALIFORNIA LILAC
RHAMNACEAE

This is another plant that is mainly known for its flowers, but which makes an excellent foliage plant for the rest of the year. It has a mass of small dark green leaves that are very heavily indented along the veins, creating a good textural effect. Several of the other evergreen species are also suitable.

CHAMAECYPARIS LAWSONIANA 'PEMBURY BLUE' ⓩ 5–9
LAWSON CYPRESS
CUPRESSACEAE

There are many coniferous trees and shrubs that make very good foliage plants. This one is a good example, with a typical conical shape, and dense foliage which has a definite blue tinge to it. The branches hang in cascades. There are many forms of Lawson cypresses, including variegated ones.

---

 height and spread   ✳ feature of interest    season of interest   *TREES AND SHRUBS* **A—C**

TREES AND SHRUBS

CONVOLVULUS CNEORUM ⓩ 8–10
CONVOLVULACEAE

This must be one of the most silver of all silver-leaved plants. It positively shines in sunlight. It is also covered in summer with white flowers that have yellow centers. It is an extremely effective plant for any foliage or mixed border. It prefers a very well-drained soil, and here it may be long-lasting; elsewhere it needs replacing every two or three years.

CORDYLINE AUSTRALIS ⓩ 10–11
AGAVACEAE

This is a splendid plant for foliage gardeners. Its sword-like leaves radiate out into almost a sphere. They create very clear-cut plants that do well as an accent or specimen plant. They are very good in containers. Under favorable conditions the plant will eventually become a tree. There are several cultivars available, some with variegated leaves.

CORNUS ALBA 'ELEGANTISSIMA' ⓩ 2–8
SILVER-VARIEGATED DOGWOOD
CORNACEAE

There is a number of *Cornus alba* cultivars that make good foliage plants, most being variegated forms. 'Elegantissima' has oval leaves with white margins, giving the shrub a very fresh look. Dogwood is also grown for its winter bark. In the case of 'Sibirica' it is bright orange-red.

CORNUS ALTERNIFOLIA ARGENTEA ⓩ 4–8
PAGODA DOGWOOD
CORNACEAE

Perhaps not as elegant in shape as *C. controversa* 'Variegata', it is its equal in foliage effect. The leaves are small and oval. They are light green with a white margin, giving the bush a very fresh appearance. It has horizontal tiers of branches but is more of a conventional bush and more suitable for a small garden.

CORNUS CONTROVERSA 'VARIEGATA' ⓩ 6–9
WEDDING CAKE TREE
CORNACEAE

The strange common name is given to this plant because of the way the horizontal branches appear in individual tiers. It is one of the most elegant of small trees and needs plenty of space to develop and to be seen. The foliage is oval, and mid-green with white margins, enhancing the beauty of the tree.

CORYLUS MAXIMA 'PURPUREA' ⓩ 4–9
PURPLE LEAF FILBERT
CORYLACEAE

A large bush grown for its dark-purple leaves. The leaves are pleated along their veins, which adds to their attraction. The bush is a mass of straight stems which should be cut to the ground every four years to rejuvenate it. The long catkins are also purple, and it produces edible cobnuts.

≣ leaf type ● light preference ⚘ speed of growth ⚙ ease of growth

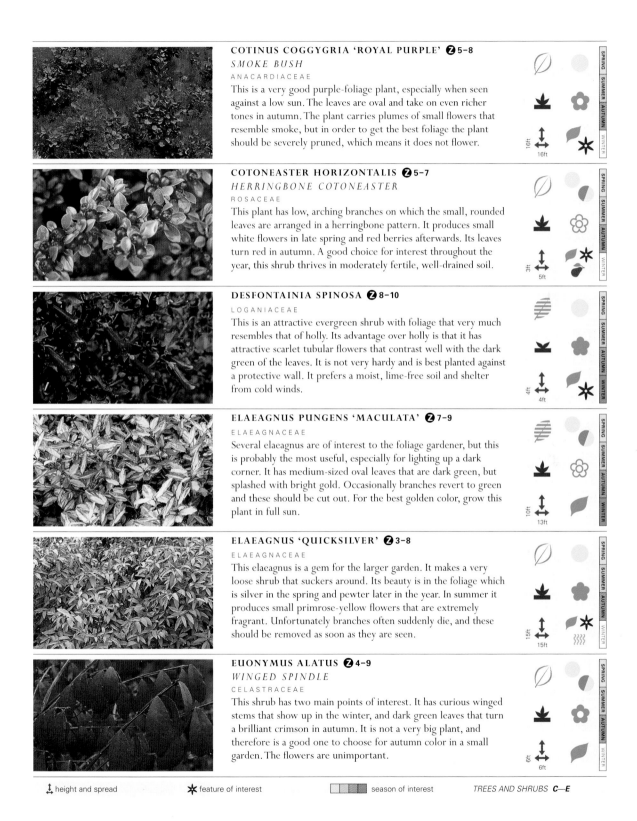

COTINUS COGGYGRIA 'ROYAL PURPLE' ❷5–8

SMOKE BUSH

ANACARDIACEAE

This is a very good purple-foliage plant, especially when seen against a low sun. The leaves are oval and take on even richer tones in autumn. The plant carries plumes of small flowers that resemble smoke, but in order to get the best foliage the plant should be severely pruned, which means it does not flower.

16ft / 16ft

COTONEASTER HORIZONTALIS ❷5–7

HERRINGBONE COTONEASTER

ROSACEAE

This plant has low, arching branches on which the small, rounded leaves are arranged in a herringbone pattern. It produces small white flowers in late spring and red berries afterwards. Its leaves turn red in autumn. A good choice for interest throughout the year, this shrub thrives in moderately fertile, well-drained soil.

3ft / 5ft

DESFONTAINIA SPINOSA ❷8–10

LOGANIACEAE

This is an attractive evergreen shrub with foliage that very much resembles that of holly. Its advantage over holly is that it has attractive scarlet tubular flowers that contrast well with the dark green of the leaves. It is not very hardy and is best planted against a protective wall. It prefers a moist, lime-free soil and shelter from cold winds.

4ft / 4ft

ELAEAGNUS PUNGENS 'MACULATA' ❷7–9

ELAEAGNACEAE

Several elaeagnus are of interest to the foliage gardener, but this is probably the most useful, especially for lighting up a dark corner. It has medium-sized oval leaves that are dark green, but splashed with bright gold. Occasionally branches revert to green and these should be cut out. For the best golden color, grow this plant in full sun.

10ft / 13ft

ELAEAGNUS 'QUICKSILVER' ❷3–8

ELAEAGNACEAE

This elaeagnus is a gem for the larger garden. It makes a very loose shrub that suckers around. Its beauty is in the foliage which is silver in the spring and pewter later in the year. In summer it produces small primrose-yellow flowers that are extremely fragrant. Unfortunately branches often suddenly die, and these should be removed as soon as they are seen.

15ft / 15ft

EUONYMUS ALATUS ❷4–9

WINGED SPINDLE

CELASTRACEAE

This shrub has two main points of interest. It has curious winged stems that show up in the winter, and dark green leaves that turn a brilliant crimson in autumn. It is not a very big plant, and therefore is a good one to choose for autumn color in a small garden. The flowers are unimportant.

6ft / 6ft

SPRING SUMMER AUTUMN WINTER

⬍ height and spread   ✳ feature of interest   ▮▮▮▮ season of interest   *TREES AND SHRUBS* **C—E**

TREES AND SHRUBS

EUONYMUS FORTUNEI ⓩ4–9
EVERGREEN BITTERSWEET
CELASTRACEAE

These are popular foliage shrubs, but are none the worse for that. The small oval leaves are green in the species but white or gold in their more common variegated forms, which brighten up dark spots. It makes excellent ground cover. Planted against a wall, the plants will creep up it.

EUONYMUS JAPONICUS ⓩ6–9
EVERGREEN EUONYMUS
CELASTRACEAE

This is a more upright bush than the previous plant. The leaves are larger but, again, it is the variegated forms, such as 'Albomarginatus' and 'Aureopictus', which are more popular. The variegated foliage has a fresh-looking quality about it which makes it very attractive.

FAGUS SYLVATICA 'RIVERSII' ⓩ5–7
COPPER BEECH
FAGACEAE

This can develop into a very big tree, when it is only suitable for big gardens, but it can be kept clipped as a hedging bush. It is slow-growing and will take sixty years or more to reach maturity. It is the classic copper beech with large, deep-purple foliage. There are other purple and variegated forms.

FATSIA JAPONICA 'VARIEGATA' ⓩ8–10
VARIEGATED JAPANESE FATSIA
ARALIACEAE

This is a shrub that makes a big impact. It has very large glossy dark green leaves that seem to make a solid mass of foliage. It has a tropical feel about it although it is hardy, which is useful for exotic-type schemes. Fatsias are very useful for shady areas. Although large, it can be controlled in smaller areas.

FUCHSIA 'GOLDEN TREASURE' ⓩ8–10
ONAGRACEAE

Fuchsias are, of course, well known as flowering plants, but there are some that also make good foliage plants. 'Golden Treasure', for example, has golden foliage. *F. magellanica* var. *gracilis* 'Variegata' has cream variegations, while *F. m.* 'Versicolor' is a mixture of pinks and grays. Fuchsias grow best in moist but well-drained soil in sun or partial shade.

GLEDITSIA TRIACANTHOS 'SUNBURST' ⓩ3–7
HONEY LOCUST
CAESALPINIACEAE

This is the tree to plant if you want a constant burst of sunshine in the garden. The foliage is a wonderful bright gold color. The leaves themselves are quite long and arching, and are composed of many leaflets, much like laburnum or wisteria. It forms a small rounded tree suitable for small gardens.

≡ leaf type   ○ light preference   ♟ speed of growth   ⚙ ease of growth

HEBE ARMSTRONGII ❷ 9–10

SCROPHULARIACEAE

One of the whipcord hebes which have foliage that looks more like that of a conifer than the majority of hebes. The individual leaves are very small and pressed tight against the stem. All the whipcords make good foliage plants. In this species the foliage is an attractive olive-green, becoming lighter in winter. It bears small white flowers in late spring and early summer.

3ft
4ft

HEBE PINGIFOLIA 'PAGEI' ❷ 8–10

SHRUBBY VERONICA

SCROPHULARIACEAE

This is a popular foliage plant for the small garden or a rock bed. It is low-growing, with attractive gray foliage that remains throughout the year. During the summer it also bears white flowers. It slowly spreads to form good ground cover. It is easily grown and needs little attention.

12in
2ft

HIPPOPHAE RHAMNOIDES ❷ 3–8

SEA BUCKTHORN

ELAEAGNACEAE

This is a good foliage plant, but only for the larger garden. It is rather untidy and has vicious spines, but this is offset by its silver foliage. The leaves are narrow. It is a particularly good plant for gardens near the sea. The flowers are insignificant, but female plants bear attractive orange berries.

16ft
16ft

HYDRANGEA ASPERA ❷ 6–9

HYDRANGEACEAE

Most hydrangeas have pleasant but not outstanding foliage. This species, however, is interesting because the leaves have a furry quality, especially on the undersides. The top is slightly furry and light green with a red edge when young, while the underside is a felted gray. The foliage can be damaged by late frosts. It prefers a moist but well-drained soil.

10ft
10ft

ILEX AQUIFOLIUM ❷ 7–9

HOLLY

AQUIFOLIACEAE

Hollies are some of the mainstays in a foliage garden. The species has dark green evergreen foliage whose prickles and gloss give it a wonderful texture and reflective quality. As well as free-standing shrubs and trees, they make good hedges. There are many good variegated cultivars.

20ft
13ft

JUNIPERUS COMMUNIS 'HIBERNICA' ❷ 2–6

IRISH JUNIPER

CUPRESSACEAE

This is a valuable conifer as it forms a vertical column and holds its shape without any need for pruning. Slender plants are not common and yet are very useful for adding vertical emphasis to a design. It is slow-growing, and does not become very tall or wide, and so is suitable for small gardens.

10ft
12in

---

 height and spread   feature of interest   ◻️◻️◻️ season of interest   *TREES AND SHRUBS E—J*

TREES AND SHRUBS

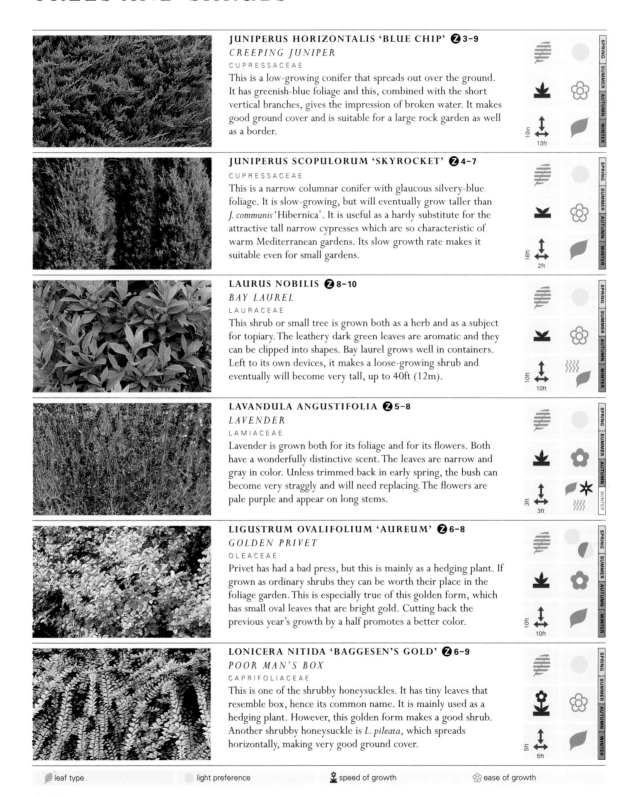

JUNIPERUS HORIZONTALIS 'BLUE CHIP' **Z** 3-9
CREEPING JUNIPER
CUPRESSACEAE

This is a low-growing conifer that spreads out over the ground. It has greenish-blue foliage and this, combined with the short vertical branches, gives the impression of broken water. It makes good ground cover and is suitable for a large rock garden as well as a border.

10in / 13ft

SPRING SUMMER AUTUMN WINTER

JUNIPERUS SCOPULORUM 'SKYROCKET' **Z** 4-7
CUPRESSACEAE

This is a narrow columnar conifer with glaucous silvery-blue foliage. It is slow-growing, but will eventually grow taller than *J. communis* 'Hibernica'. It is useful as a hardy substitute for the attractive tall narrow cypresses which are so characteristic of warm Mediterranean gardens. Its slow growth rate makes it suitable even for small gardens.

16ft / 2ft

SPRING SUMMER AUTUMN WINTER

LAURUS NOBILIS **Z** 8-10
BAY LAUREL
LAURACEAE

This shrub or small tree is grown both as a herb and as a subject for topiary. The leathery dark green leaves are aromatic and they can be clipped into shapes. Bay laurel grows well in containers. Left to its own devices, it makes a loose-growing shrub and eventually will become very tall, up to 40ft (12m).

10ft / 10ft

SPRING SUMMER AUTUMN WINTER

LAVANDULA ANGUSTIFOLIA **Z** 5-8
LAVENDER
LAMIACEAE

Lavender is grown both for its foliage and for its flowers. Both have a wonderfully distinctive scent. The leaves are narrow and gray in color. Unless trimmed back in early spring, the bush can become very straggly and will need replacing. The flowers are pale purple and appear on long stems.

3ft / 3ft

SPRING SUMMER AUTUMN WINTER

LIGUSTRUM OVALIFOLIUM 'AUREUM' **Z** 6-8
GOLDEN PRIVET
OLEACEAE

Privet has had a bad press, but this is mainly as a hedging plant. If grown as ordinary shrubs they can be worth their place in the foliage garden. This is especially true of this golden form, which has small oval leaves that are bright gold. Cutting back the previous year's growth by a half promotes a better color.

10ft / 10ft

SPRING SUMMER AUTUMN WINTER

LONICERA NITIDA 'BAGGESEN'S GOLD' **Z** 6-9
POOR MAN'S BOX
CAPRIFOLIACEAE

This is one of the shrubby honeysuckles. It has tiny leaves that resemble box, hence its common name. It is mainly used as a hedging plant. However, this golden form makes a good shrub. Another shrubby honeysuckle is *L. pileata*, which spreads horizontally, making very good ground cover.

5ft / 5ft

SPRING SUMMER AUTUMN WINTER

---

leaf type   light preference   speed of growth   ease of growth

MAHONIA JAPONICA ⓩ 7–8
BERBERIDACEAE

Nearly all the mahonias, of which this is but a representative, make excellent foliage plants. They have leaves a bit like large holly leaves, although they are flatter and the spines are not so vicious. The leaves are green but often take on a reddish tinge, particularly in autumn. They all have yellow flowers in winter. Mahonias prefer a moist soil.

MUSA BASJOO ⓩ 8–10
BANANA
MUSACEAE

A truly exotic plant with enormous leaves. These are 36in (90cm) or longer and arch from the top of the trunk. They are slightly tender but generally survive in sheltered places in the garden. These take a lot of beating for jungle-foliage effect, especially when planted with bamboos and other large-leaved plants.

NANDINA DOMESTICA ⓩ 6–9
HEAVENLY BAMBOO
BERBERIDACEAE

In spite of its common name, this is not a bamboo but a shrub with straight upright shoots that look a bit like bamboo. The leaves are composed of leaflets which turn red during winter. It has white flowers and clusters of bright red berries, which remain all winter.

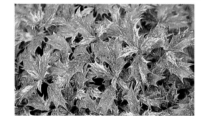

OSMANTHUS HETEROPHYLLUS 'VARIEGATUS' ⓩ 7–9
HOLLY OSMANTHUS
OLEACEAE

As the common name suggests, this foliage plant has leaves that closely resemble holly. It is not so prickly and is used as a shrub rather than hedging. It has insignificant but fragrant flowers in late autumn. There are several variegated forms, such as this, which are more interesting than the species.

OZOTHAMNUS ROSMARINIFOLIUS ⓩ 8–9
ASTERACEAE

This is an evergreen shrub with an upright habit and foliage which is very similar to that of rosemary. The leaves are needle-like and dark green, which contrasts well with the silvery stems. In early summer, it produces clusters of fragrant white flowers that are red in bud before they open. It needs a warm position, sheltered from cold winds.

PHILADELPHUS CORONARIUS 'AUREUS' ⓩ 5–8
GOLDEN PHILADELPHUS
HYDRANGEACEAE

Most philadelphus are grown for their scented flowers, but this variety is grown for its superb foliage. It is a golden color, turning greener in summer. It burns in strong sun so should be planted in dappled shade, which it illuminates as if it were in the sun. It carries white scented flowers in summer.

---

 height and spread   ✳ feature of interest   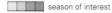 season of interest   *TREES AND SHRUBS* **J—P**

TREES AND SHRUBS

PICEA PUNGENS 'GLOBOSA' **Z** 3-8

PINACEAE

The beauty of this dwarf spruce is that it is very slow-growing and makes an ideal conifer for the small garden or for the rock garden. The foliage is blue-gray, and it forms a compact rounded shrub. *P. pungens* 'Montgomery' is very similar in appearance and growth rate. Grow in a deep, moist, but well-drained, ideally neutral to acid soil in full sun.

3ft / 3ft

SPRING SUMMER AUTUMN WINTER

PINUS WALLICHIANA **Z** 6-9

BHUTAN PINE

PINACEAE

A number of pines make good foliage plants, especially as they contrast so strongly with most other types of foliage. In this particular case the needles are long and hang down in large, soft-looking clusters, creating a superb texture. It is also known by several other names, including *P. griffithii*.

60ft / 30ft

SPRING SUMMER AUTUMN WINTER

PRUNUS CERASIFERA 'NIGRA' **Z** 5-9

ROSACEAE

This cherry is valuable to the foliage gardener because of its deep purple foliage. When young the leaves are red, darkening as the season progresses. It is one of only a handful of really good purple-leaved trees. It is small enough for the small garden. It has complementary pink flowers in spring. It prefers a moist but well-drained soil.

25ft / 25ft

SPRING SUMMER AUTUMN WINTER

PYRUS SALICIFOLIA 'PENDULA' **Z** 5-9

WEEPING PEAR

ROSACEAE

This one of the classic silver-leaved plants. There are several forms, but the best one is an upright tree with weeping branches which create a cascade of silver. In other forms, the main leader also droops. The leaves are a good silver through the growing season. It has white flowers.

20ft / 15ft

SPRING SUMMER AUTUMN WINTER

RHAMNUS ALATERNUS 'ARGENTEOVARIEGATA' **Z** 7-9

ITALIAN BUCKTHORN

RHAMNACEAE

This is a good foliage garden plant. It forms a large dense bush with a conical habit that is covered with small to medium oval leaves. They are leathery in texture, and in color are an underlying gray-green edged with a creamy-white variegation. They lighten a dark spot.

10ft / 10ft

SPRING SUMMER AUTUMN WINTER

RHODODENDRON LANATUM **Z** 2-11

ERICACEAE

Most rhododendrons make reasonable foliage plants, even if they are only for background use. However, the majority are not top-flight plants, but among them are a few that can be grown for their foliage. This particular species, for example, has white furry leaves that turn deep red-brown as they age. All rhododendrons require a rich, moist, but well-drained, acid soil.

13ft / 13ft

SPRING SUMMER AUTUMN WINTER

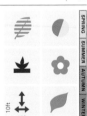

🍃 leaf type   ⬤ light preference   ⚲ speed of growth   ✿ ease of growth

ROBINIA PSEUDOACACIA 'FRISIA' ❷ 4–9
FALSE ACACIA
PAPILIONACEAE

'Frisia' is a tree whose foliage can be used to create a bright spot in a garden. The leaves are a fresh lime-yellow darkening to yellow as the year progresses. The leaves are like those of wisteria, divided into leaflets. It has clusters of white flowers, also like a wisteria, in midsummer.

ROMNEYA COULTERI ❷ 7–9
TREE POPPY
PAPAVERACEAE

Sometimes considered a perennial, the real delight of this plant is the white poppy-like flowers, but it also makes a very credible foliage plant. The leaves are silvery-gray. They are deeply divided and appear on a series of upright and arching stems in an open bush. The plant suckers.

ROSA GLAUCA ❷ 2–8
ROSACEAE

Roses, on the whole, are not considered as foliage plants in spite of a few having fine glossy leaves. The one exception is this which has glaucous-gray leaves with a touch of pink in them. Bigger leaves can be produced by severely pruning it each spring. It produces small complementary pink flowers in summer, followed by spherical red hips in autumn.

ROSMARINUS OFFICINALIS ❷ 8–10
ROSEMARY
LAMIACEAE

Rosemary is an evergreen herb that is worth growing in any garden. The leaves are short and needle-like, green on top and silver below. It is very fragrant when touched, making it worth planting near a path so it can be caressed in passing. The flowers are blue and appear in spring.

SALIX BABYLONICA ❷ 6–9
WEEPING WILLOW
SALICACEAE

This is a tree to treat with caution. It is very attractive, especially when it grows large, and therein lies the problem; it does get very big, and is not suitable for small gardens or near buildings. As a tree by a large pond, it is second to none, however, with its sweeping branches of light green foliage.

SALIX LANATA ❷ 3–5
WOOLLY WILLOW
SALICACEAE

As a group, many of the willows are worth growing for the foliage garden, especially the various silver-leaved ones. This silver-leaved one is smaller than most others and is suitable for a small garden or large rock garden. The leaves are furry, *S. exigua* is a good example of a larger shrub.

---

 height and spread   feature of interest   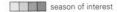 season of interest   *TREES AND SHRUBS* **P—S**

TREES AND SHRUBS

SALVIA OFFICINALIS 'ICTERINA' Z5–8

VARIEGATED SAGE

LAMIACEAE

Sage itself is not over-pleasing as a foliage plant, but this variegared form is very attractive. The slightly furry leaves have a fresh-looking quality about them when young, as does the purple-leaved form 'Purpurascens'. Both are short-lived and need replacing every few years.

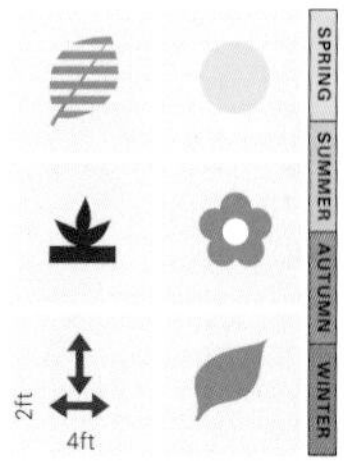
2ft
4ft
SPRING
SUMMER
AUTUMN
WINTER

SAMBUCUS NIGRA F. LACINIATA Z6–8

CUT-LEAVED ELDER

CAPRIFOLIACEAE

A number of the elders have good foliage. This is one of the best. It has large green leaves that are very deeply cut, almost fern-like, creating an interesting textural quality. It is best to cut the plant back each year to promote larger leaves. If left unpruned it produces very large flat heads of white flowers.

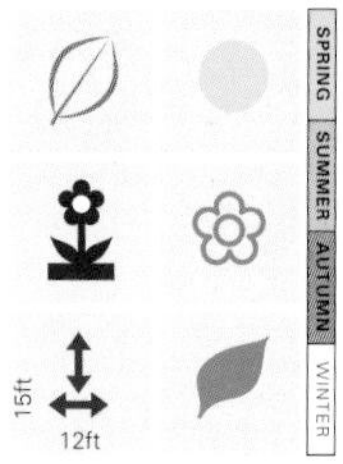
15ft
12ft
SPRING
SUMMER
AUTUMN
WINTER

SAMBUCUS RACEMOSA 'PLUMOSA AUREA' Z3–7

RED-BERRIED ELDER

CAPRIFOLIACEAE

There are several good golden or variegated forms of elder, of which this is one of the best. It forms a bush rather than a tree and has golden leaves which are flushed with bronze when they are young. Cutting hard back each winter helps to produce good foliage, but at the expense of flowers.

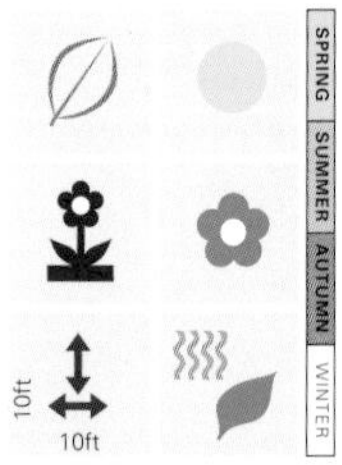
10ft
10ft
SPRING
SUMMER
AUTUMN
WINTER

SANTOLINA PINNATA SUBSP. NEAPOLITANA Z9–10

ASTERACEAE

This plant and *S. chamaecyparissus* (cotton lavender) are two mainstays of the mixed border when bushy silver foliage is required. The leaves are small, creating a feathery look, and are aromatic. Both plants have bright yellow flowers in summer, which are usually removed by most gardeners. They need trimming in spring, to promote fresh new foliage.

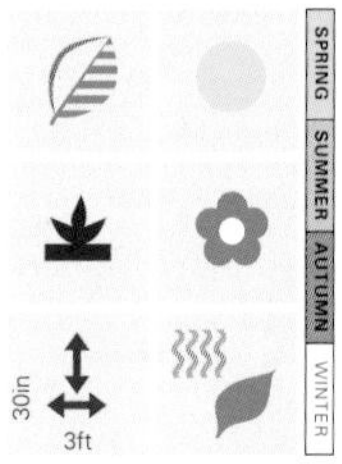
30in
3ft
SPRING
SUMMER
AUTUMN
WINTER

TAMARIX RAMOSISSIMA Z3–8

TAMARISK

TAMARICACEAE

Also known as *T. pentandra*, this shrub is usually grown for its autumn plumes of pink flowers, but it also has interesting foliage, especially for gardens near the sea where choice of plants is limited. The leaves are a glabrous blue-green. It is a graceful shrub with light airy arching stems.

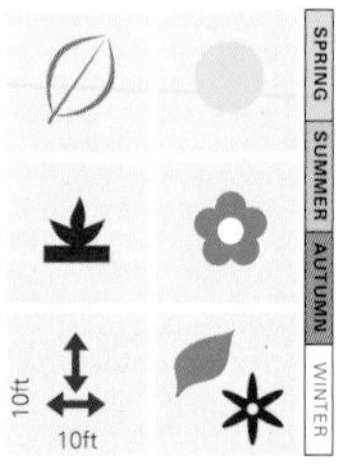
10ft
10ft
SPRING
SUMMER
AUTUMN
WINTER

TAXUS BACCATA AUREA GROUP Z7–8

GOLDEN YEW

TAXACEAE

Yew is invaluable as a foliage plant, even if only as the best of all hedging materials. It creates a most marvelous background. This is the golden form, which is generally gold-flushed rather than totally golden. They make good specimen shrubs or can be used to provide variation in a hedge.

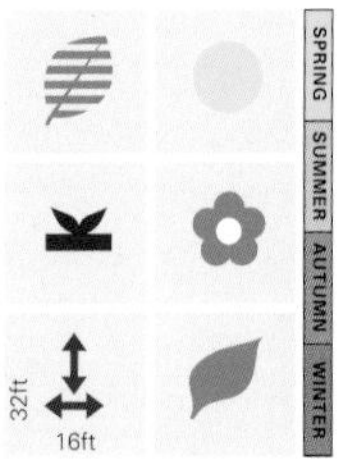
32ft
16ft
SPRING
SUMMER
AUTUMN
WINTER

leaf type | light preference | speed of growth | ease of growth

THUJA ORIENTALIS 'AUREA NANA' ❷ 6-9
CUPRESSACEAE

This is a beautiful conifer with vertical foliage creating waves of color. The foliage is gold on the outer layers with a greener shade glimpsed inside the compact bush, producing an attractive effect. It is slow-growing and never becomes very large, making it an ideal conifer for a small garden. It prefers a moist but well-drained soil, and needs shelter from cold winds.

THYMUS SERPYLLUM ❷ 4-9
THYME
LAMIACEAE

One of the small shrubby thymes grown for its foliage, this forms a creeping mat, covered in small aromatic leaves. The species has green leaves but there are several varieties with silver or golden variegation. It is a good foliage plant for planting in paving as it is tough enough to withstand being walked on.

TRACHYCARPUS FORTUNEI ❷ 9-10
CHUSAN PALM
ARECACEAE

A slightly untidy-looking shrub or tree that is valuable because of its large fans of sword-like leaves, up to 36in (90cm) across. This is the hardiest of the palms, but still requires a sheltered spot. It can be used to help create exotic foliage effects. It must be grown in a free-draining position.

VIBURNUM DAVIDII ❷ 8-9
CAPRIFOLIACEAE

On the whole, viburnums do not make good foliage plants except for their autumn color. This species, however, is an exception. It has large oval leaves that are dark green in color and ribbed with very prominent veins, which give it a strong textural quality. Female plants carry small white flowers followed by attractive blue berries.

VINCA MINOR ❷ 4-9
PERIWINKLE
APOCYNACEAE

This plant is not in the first league of foliage plants, but it has the advantage of making good ground cover in shady places and so earns its place. The small oval leaves are mid- to dark green and appear on long arching stems. It bears blue-purple flowers. There are several variegated forms, including 'Aureovariegata.'

WEIGELA FLORIDA 'VARIEGATA' ❷ 5-8
CAPRIFOLIACEAE

Weigelas are normally grown for their flowers, but several can also hold their own as foliage plants. This variety has attractive variegated green leaves edged with creamy white. The pretty pink bell-shaped flowers appear in late spring and early summer. Another good form is 'Foliis Purpureis' which has interesting bronze-green colored leaves.

↕ height and spread   ✳ feature of interest   ▦ season of interest   *TREES AND SHRUBS* **S—W**

CLIMBERS

ACTINIDIA KOLOMIKTA ⓩ 5–8
ACTINIDIACEAE

This climber is closely related to the kiwi fruit, but in this case it is grown for its foliage. The coloring and freshness of the leaves are quite unusual. They are oval and basically dark green, but the upper half or more of the leaf is often white, which ages to pink, giving all three colors on one leaf. In summer, it bears insignificant white flowers, followed by yellow-green fruits.

CLEMATIS MONTANA ⓩ 6–9
RANUCULACEAE

This is a climber that is mainly known for the masses of pink flowers it produces in spring. However, it is also a good foliage plant, especially for creating thick curtains of leaves, which are tinged with purple. It is a vigorous climber that will soon cover its supports, and is useful for hiding eyesores. It prefers a sheltered site with a well-drained soil.

FALLOPIA BALDSCHUANICA ⓩ 5–9
RUSSIAN VINE
POLYGONACEAE

Another name for this plant is mile-a-minute, and that sums it up. It is a rampant climber suitable for covering trees or eyesores. The foliage is light green, fading to yellow, and eventually offering a good yellowy-bronze autumn color. It is covered in clouds of creamy flowers in late summer.

HEDERA COLCHICA ⓩ 5–10
PERSIAN IVY
ARALIACEAE

This is an ivy for producing good cover. It has much bigger leaves than the common ivy. Although there are green forms it is usually the variegated ones that are most grown, in particular 'Sulphur Heart'. This has bright green leaves with bright gold central variegation. It also makes good ground cover.

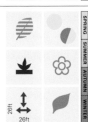

HEDERA HELIX ⓩ 5–10
COMMON IVY
ARALIACEAE

The common ivy has very many cultivars, although there is not a great deal of difference between them. This is an excellent evergreen climber that is suitable for walls, trees, fences, or ground cover. As well as various shapes of the ordinary green variety, there are also numerous variegated forms.

HUMULUS LUPULUS 'AUREUS' ⓩ 4–8
GOLDEN HOP
CANNABACEAE

This is one of the few herbaceous climbers for the foliage garden. It is grown for its golden foliage and in female clones for the yellow-green hops. It is a twining plant that grows up poles, wires, trees, or hedges. The dead stems and foliage need to be cut to the ground in autumn.

🌿 leaf type	🔵 light preference	🌱 speed of growth	⚙ ease of growth

HYDRANGEA ANOMALA SUBSP. PETIOLARIS ❷4–9
CLIMBING HYDRANGEA
HYDRANGEACEAE

A self-clinging climber that is much used for covering walls. It can also be used to grow through trees in the manner of ivy. The leaves are broadly oval and are light green, changing to yellow in autumn. It has white flowers. It can be a nuisance, getting under roof tiles, and should be cut back to gutter level.

LONICERA JAPONICA 'AUREORETICULATA' ❷4–10
JAPANESE HONEYSUCKLE
CAPRIFOLIACEAE

Honeysuckles do not usually make good foliage plants. One of the few exceptions is this one. It has oval leaves that are bright green with the veins picked out in gold, sometimes with the areas between flushed also with gold. The flowers are small, yellow, and fragrant. It is sometimes evergreen.

PARTHENOCISSUS HENRYANA ❷7–8
CHINESE VIRGINIA CREEPER
VITACEAE

All the parthenocissus make good wall-covering plants, but this is arguably the best. It has fresh-looking foliage, each leaf consisting of usually five leaflets. The leaves are bright green with a distinctive white midrib and veining. They all have very good autumn color. It can be rampant.

VITIS COIGNETIAE ❷5–9
CRIMSON GLORY VINE
VITACEAE

This has one of the largest leaves of all climbers. They are up to 12in (30cm) across and heart-shaped. In summer they are mid-green, but in autumn they take on a very brilliant red color. It is an excellent plant for growing over pergolas and arbors. It will grow in a wide variety of conditions.

VITIS VINIFERA 'PURPUREA' ❷6–9
PURPLE-LEAVED GRAPE
VITACEAE

This is a variety of the ordinary grape that is grown for its foliage rather than the fruit. The leaves are lobed, and, as the name suggests, purple. When young the leaves are greener but they have an attractive metallic sheen to them. They have good autumn color. It is good for pergolas and arbors.

WISTERIA SINENSIS ❷5–8
PAPILIONACEAE

Wisteria is not generally thought of as a foliage plant, but for most of the growing season that is just what it is. It produces a mass of attractive light to mid-green leaves, each of which comprises a number of leaflets. It can be grown against walls or over pergolas. It can even be grown as a standard tree. It prefers a moist but well-drained soil.

 height and spread   ✳ feature of interest   ▬▬▬ season of interest   *CLIMBERS A—W*

GLOSSARY

ALPINE: A plant that in its natural mountain habitat grows above the uppermost limit of trees. More colloquially, plants that are suitable for rock gardens are called alpines.

ANNUAL: A plant that grows from seed, flowers, and dies within the same year. Some half-hardy perennial plants are used as annuals, that is, they die off in the winter.

AQUATIC PLANT: A plant that lives totally or partly submerged in water.

AXIL: The upper angle between leaf and stem.

BEDDING PLANTS: Plants that are set out for a temporary seasonal displays and discarded at the end of the season.

BIENNIAL: A plant raised from seed that makes its initial growth in one year and flowers during the following one, then dies.

BOG GARDEN PLANTS: Plants that live with their roots in moist soil.

BULB: An underground food storage organ formed of fleshy, modified leaves that enclose a dormant shoot.

CALYX: The outer and protective part of a flower. It is usually green and is very apparent in roses.

COMPOST: Vegetable waste from kitchens, as well as soft parts of garden plants, which is encouraged to decompose and to form a material that can be dug into soil or used to create a mulch around plants.

CORM: An underground storage organ formed of a swollen stem base, for example, a gladiolus.

CULTIVAR: A shortened term for "cultivated variety" that indicates a variety raised in cultivation. Strictly speaking, most modern varieties are cultivars, but the term variety is still widely used because it is familiar to most gardeners.

CUTTING: A section of plant which is detached and encouraged to form roots and stems to provide a new independent plant. Cuttings may be taken from roots, stems, or leaves.

DEAD-HEADING: The removal of a faded flower head to prevent the formation of seeds and to encourage the development of further flowers.

DORMANT: When a plant is alive but is making no growth, it is called dormant. The dormant period is usually the winter.

EVERGREEN: Plants that appear to be green throughout the year and not to lose their leaves are called evergreen. In reality, however, they shed some of their leaves throughout the year, while producing others.

FRIABLE: Soil that is crumbly and light and easily worked. It especially applies to soil being prepared as a seedbed in spring.

HALF-HARDY: A plant that can withstand fairly low temperatures, but needs protection from frost.

HALF-HARDY ANNUAL: An annual that is sown in gentle warmth in a greenhouse in spring, the seedlings being transferred to wider spacings in pots or boxes. The plants are placed in a garden or container only when all risk of frost has passed.

HARDEN OFF: To gradually accustom plants to cooler conditions so that they can be planted outside.

HARDY: A plant that is able to survive outdoors in winter. In the case of some rock-garden plants, good drainage is essential to ensure their survival.

HERB: A plant that is grown for its aromatic qualities and can often be used in cooking or medicinally.

HERBACEOUS PERENNIAL: A plant with no woody tissue that lives for several years. Herbaceous perennials may be deciduous or evergreen.

HYBRID: A cross between two different species, varieties, or genera of plants.

LOAM: Friable mixture of sand, silt and clay.

MARGINAL PLANTS: Plants that live in shallow water at the edges of ponds. Some also thrive in boggy soil surrounding a pond.

MULCHING: Covering the soil around plants with well-decayed organic material such as garden compost, peat or, in the case of rock garden plants, stone chippings, or ¼ in(6mm) shingle.

NEUTRAL: Soil that is neither acid nor alkaline, with a pH of 7.0, is said to be neutral. Most plants grow in a pH of about 6.5.

PEAT: A naturally occurring substance formed from partly rotted organic material in waterlogged soils, used as a growing medium and soil additive.

PERENNIAL: Any plant that lives for three or more years is called a perennial.

PERGOLA: An open timber structure made up of linked arches.

POTTING COMPOST: Traditionally, a compost formed of loam, sharp sand and peat, fertilizers, and chalk. The ratio of the ingredients is altered according to whether the compost is used for sowing seeds, potting-up, or repotting plants into larger containers. Recognition of the environmental importance of conserving peat beds has led to many modern composts being formed of other organic materials, such as coir or shredded bark.

PRICKING OUT: Transplanting seedlings from the container in which they were sown to one where they are more widely spaced.

RACEME: An elongated flower head with each flower having a stem.

RAISED BED: A raised area, that is encircled by a wall or other barrier. Rock garden plants can be grown both in the raised bed and the wall.

RHIZOME: An underground or partly buried horizontal stem. They can be slender or fleshy. Some irises have thick, fleshy rhizomes, while those of lily-of-the-valley are slender and creeping. They act as storage organs and perpetuate plants from one season to another.

SCREE BED: An area formed of layers of rubble, gravel and compost, imitating naturally occurring areas of scree.

SEED LEAVES: The first leaves that develop on a seedling, which are coarser and more robust than the true leaves.

SEMI-EVERGREEN: A plant that may keep some of its leaves in a reasonably mild winter.

SINK GARDENS: Old stone sinks partly filled with drainage material and then with freely draining compost. They are planted with miniature conifers and bulbs, as well as small rock garden plants. These features are usually displayed on terraces and patios.

SPECIES ROSE: A term that is used for a wild rose or one of its near relatives.

STAMEN: The male part of a flower.

STANDARD: A tree or shrub trained to form a rounded head of branches at the top of a clear stem.

SUB-SHRUB: Small and spreading shrub with a woody base. It differs from normal shrubs in that when grown in temperate regions its upper stems and shoots die back during winter.

TENDER: A plant which will not tolerate temperatures below freezing is referred to as tender.

TOPSOIL: The uppermost layer of soil which is structured and contains organic matter and humus.

TUBER: A swollen, thickened, and fleshy stem or root. Some tubers are swollen roots (dahlia), while others are swollen stems (potato). They serve as storage organs and help to perpetuate plants from one season to another.

VARIEGATED: Usually applied to leaves and used to describe a state of having two or more colors.

VARIETY: A naturally occurring variation of a species that retains its characteristics when propagated. The term is often used for cultivars.

WILDLIFE POND: An informal pond, often positioned towards the far end of a garden, which encourages the presence of wildlife such as frogs, birds, insects, and small mammals.

INDEX

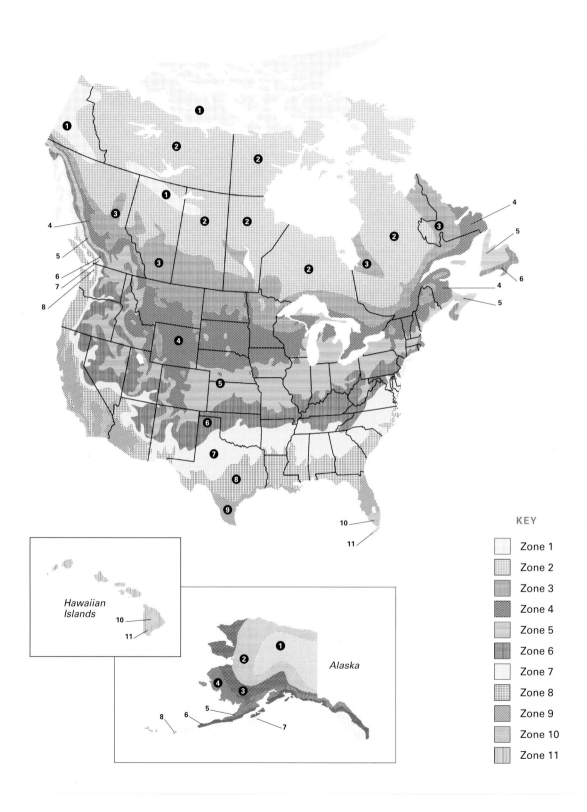

KEY

Zone 1
Zone 2
Zone 3
Zone 4
Zone 5
Zone 6
Zone 7
Zone 8
Zone 9
Zone 10
Zone 11

Hawaiian Islands

Alaska

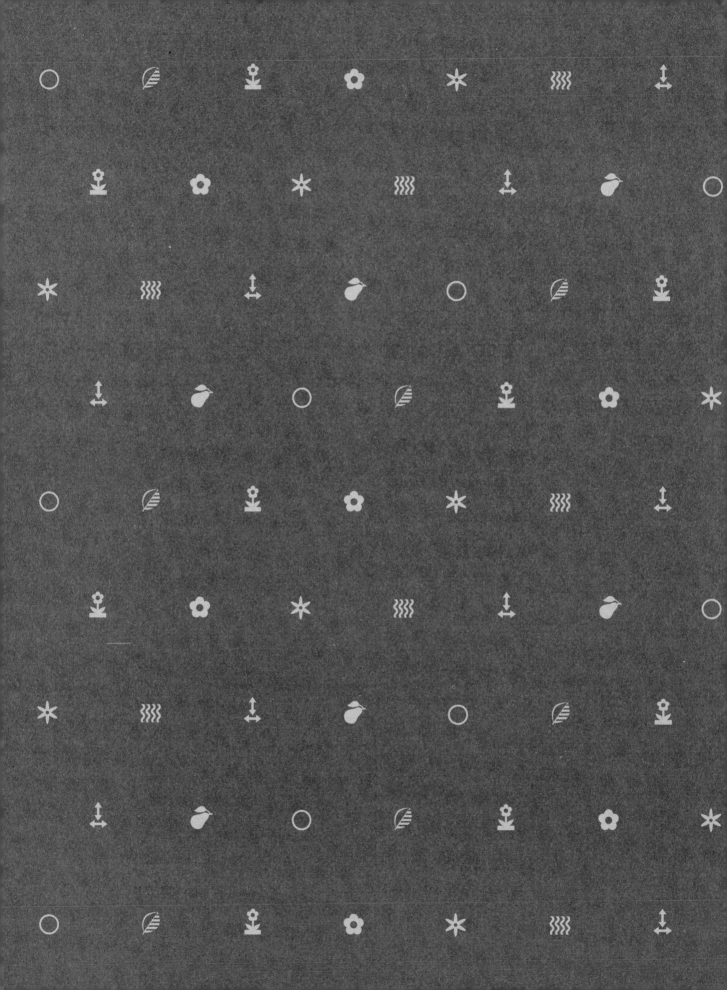